A Short History of the Mass

A SHORT
HISTORY OF THE
Mass

ALFRED MCBRIDE, O. PRAEM.

ST. ANTHONY MESSENGER PRESS
Cincinnati, Ohio

RESCRIPT

In accord with the *Code of Canon Law*, I hereby grant my permission to publish *A Short History of the Mass*, by Alfred McBride, O.Praem.
Most Reverend Carl K. Moeddel
Vicar General and Auxiliary Bishop of the Archdiocese of Cincinnati
Cincinnati, Ohio
July 24, 2006

The permission to publish is a declaration that a book or pamphlet is considered to be free from doctrinal or moral error. It is not implied that those who have granted the permission to publish agree with the contents, opinions or statements expressed.

Excerpts from the English translation of the *Catechism of the Catholic Church* for the United States of America, copyright ©1994, United States Catholic Conference, Inc.— Libreria Editrice Vaticana. English translation of the: *Catechism of the Catholic Church Modifications from the Editio Typica,* copyright ©1997, United States Catholic Conference, Inc.—Libreria Editrice Vaticana. Used with permission.

The illustration credits on page 128 constitute an extension of this copyright page.

Scripture passages have been taken from *New Revised Standard Version Bible,* copyright ©1989 by the Division of Christian Education of the National Council of the Churches of Christ in the U.S.A., and used by permission. All rights reserved.

Cover and book design by Mark Sullivan
Cover photo: Erich Lessing/Art Resource, NY
Leonardo da Vinci: Jesus and apostles, from Leonardo's Last Supper, 1498.

LIBRARY OF CONGRESS CATALOGING-IN-PUBLICATION DATA
McBride, Alfred.
A short history of the Mass / Alfred McBride.
p. cm.
ISBN-13: 978-0-86716-744-3 (pbk. : alk. paper)
ISBN-10: 0-86716-744-0 (pbk. : alk. paper) 1. Lord's Supper—History. 2. Mass—History. I. Title.

BV823.M387 2006
264'.0203609—dc22

2006024697

ISBN-13: 978-0-86716-744-3
ISBN-10: 0-86716-744-0

Published by St. Anthony Messenger Press.
28 W. Liberty St.
Cincinnati, OH 45202
www.AmericanCatholic.org

Printed in the United States of America.
Printed on acid-free paper.

06 07 08 09 10 5 4 3 2 1

contents

• • • • • • • • • • •

introduction

. . . .

I have been able to celebrate Holy
Mass in chapels built along moun-
tain paths, on lakeshores and sea-
coasts; I have celebrated it on
altars built in stadiums and in city
squares.... This varied scenario of
celebrations of the Eucharist has
given me a powerful experience of
its universal and, so to speak, cosmic character. Yes, cosmic!
Because even when it is celebrated
on the humble altar of a country
church, the Eucharist is always in
some way celebrated on the altar
of the world. It unites heaven and
earth. It embraces and permeates
all creation.

—POPE JOHN PAUL II, *ECCLESIA DE
EUCHARISTIA*, 8

I t is a very human trait to treasure the last words of a dying
person. Such words seem to summarize the character of the
individual. In the case of Pope John Paul II, his encyclical
Ecclesia de Eucharistia aptly captures the heart of this great
priest. He used the last year of his life to awaken in the universal church a new appreciation of the Eucharist. His
encyclical inaugurated the Year of the Eucharist. Providentially, the

first trip of his successor Pope Benedict XVI was to Bari, Italy, to preach at a national Eucharistic Congress.

This occasion also seemed to me to be a motivation to write this book on the history of the Mass, an idea that has been on my mind for many years. Long ago, on March 12, 1976, I delivered an address to the assembly of the bishops and major superiors of men and women of New England on the history of the Eucharist. I only had one hour to accomplish this and much of what I said was mostly a sketch. Cardinal Humberto Medeiros was present and said to me afterward he liked the presentation since he had himself written a study of that history early in his life.

I thought then that maybe I should turn the material into a full-length book but always had other immediate needs to face. In retrospect, I am glad I waited thirty years to devote a year to this topic. This was a good time to reflect on the Mass, which by now had attained reasonable stability after the experiments that followed Vatican II. Generations of new Catholics whose only experience of Mass is post–Vatican II, along with veteran Catholics, might be ready for a global look at how the Mass journeyed from the Upper Room to American suburbia and contemporary urban life—from the hands of Christ to the local twenty-first-century priest.

I was not inclined to write a long book that traveled the byways of crises and exceptions and detailed development. I prefer the forest a little more than the trees. I think the big picture is most pastorally useful for the busy Catholic who might like to know the story though not inclined to take up and read Joseph Jungmann's vast and magnificent *Mass of the Roman Rite*. Still, I would be thrilled if this small study in fact promoted the motivation to read his great work.

It seems to me that the value of a history of the Mass is, first, to illustrate the challenges faced by the apostles and the bishops who followed them in the early church to translate the Lord's Supper into a eucharistic celebration not accompanied by a Passover or Sabbath meal. They restructured the Mass with an adaptation of the synagogue word service plus a beautifully developed Eucharistic Prayer. More remarkably, they did this within a generation after the Resurrection of Christ. The Holy Spirit was living and active among them. Despite all the vagaries of the centuries thereafter, that basic structure has survived and is still the "bones" of today's liturgy.

Speaking of historical shifts, I was impressed by the transition of the church after Constantine from a Mass linked to house liturgies to one celebrated in a church building. Even when this was a massive one such as a Roman basilica, the church carefully preserved the values of the previous approach. They did not tamper with the fundamental structure of liturgy of Word and liturgy of Eucharist.

The celebrant continued to dress as he did at home Masses. Eventually, the vesture of the priest became "vestments" since the celebrant did not change what he wore, while male clothing fashions went on to other styles. Every effort was made to involve the participants in the service. In the churches of the east, the central-plan style of building facilitated involvement since it brought the people into relative intimacy with the altar.

When I came to the medieval period that saw the removal of the people from formal participation in the Eucharist due to their not knowing Latin or to the separation of the nave from the altar by choir stalls (and even walls) and by other matters, I felt a need to remind readers that the majority of Catholics were parishioners of the fabled village churches in rural settings. The smallness of the congregation and size of the churches and the communal awareness of small town life provided a sense of belonging to the Eucharist that may have been missing in great monastic churches or those run by cathedral canons. I was inspired by Eamon Duffy's wonderful evocation of this form of parish life in England before the Reformation in his book *The Stripping of the Altars*. In other words, God's people found another way to draw strength from the Mass.

I sought a similar counterpoint when reviewing the Mass of the era after the Council of Trent. The rise of baroque architecture with its new openness to the altar drew the people back into the setting of the celebration. Musical geniuses such as Palestrina and Mozart provided church choirs with unforgettable Masses. Still, the kind of participation the early church had and we now enjoy was missing.

For my next counterpoint, I turned to the wonderful spiritual resources provided by Saint Ignatius of Loyola, Saint Francis de Sales and the Carmelites Saint Teresa of Avila and Saint John of the Cross who made possible a presence at Mass of countless numbers of people who were developing an admirable inner life with Christ. Such worshipers came disposed to the graces of the Mass and were nourished richly with the Eucharist.

In other words, I saw that the Holy Spirit led people to find various ways to benefit from the incomparable treasure of the Mass. While I prefer what the Spirit has given us in our own time as the way to be involved in the Mass, I never cease to be awed that no matter what the style of belonging to the Eucharist, the Catholic people stayed with the Eucharist through thick and thin, sometimes giving their lives as was the case of Catholics in Reformation England and in evolutionary France and in Communist-run Eastern Europe.

When I came to the last chapter that dealt with the Mass after Vatican II and the liturgical movement that led up to it, I remembered my seminary days at St. Norbert Abbey in De Pere, Wisconsin, where we were excited by the new thinking about the liturgy that we read about in the Benedictine magazine *Orate Fratres* as well as in the proceedings of the national liturgical congresses. I found the commentaries on the liturgy by Dom Prosper Guéranger and the Klosterneuberg Canon Pius Parsch absorbing and life changing. When Monsignor Martin Hellriegel gave our priests a liturgical retreat, I realized in a very personal way the future of the liturgy. It was not hard for me to expect that the very first document published by Vatican II would be on the liturgy of the church, which it was.

In reviewing the liturgical changes created after the Council, I particularly enjoyed contrasting the elements that disappeared with the ones that replaced them. I did have much interest in the argumentative aspects of the changes and subsequent developments. My generation and the one just following seem to savor such battles and finds endless ways to recycle them. While some historians should keep a record, I did not feel such a responsibility.

I am comfortable with the fact that the Vatican has an Office of Divine Worship and the Sacraments mandated to monitor liturgical practice and development. Its leadership has the staff to research these issues and the advantage of being at the focal point of the universal church. I guess at heart I am fundamentally a catechist dedicated to taking the message and massaging it in a way that it becomes accessible to parishioners.

I am grateful to Lisa Biedenbach who keeps motivating me to write and who found this subject an appealing one for the publisher. I am also grateful to the staff of St. Anthony Messenger Press who have been good friends of mine since I began writing for them in 1981. Bless them. And may God bless you, too, for your interest in the history of the Mass.

Father Alfred McBride, O.PRAEM.
St. Joseph Priory, De Pere, Wisconsin

chapter one

· · · · · · · · · · ·

THE
LAST
SUPPER

No one can fully express the sweetness of this sacrament, in which spiritual delight is tasted at its very source, and in which we renew the memory of that surpassing love for us which Christ revealed in his passion.

—SAINT THOMAS AQUINAS, FROM THE
OFFICE OF READINGS FOR THE FEAST OF
CORPUS CHRISTI

Pope John Paul II frequently returned to the events of the Last Supper. Read his numerous Holy Thursday letters to his brother priests and his encyclical on the Eucharist, *Ecclesia de Eucharistia*—The Church of the Eucharist. He believed in returning again and again to the source of this sacrament that contains the entire treasure of the church. His prayerful faith always found fresh ways to bring the wonder and beauty of the Eucharist alive through his contemplation of that historic moment in Christ's saving work on our behalf. He urged us to share the amazement he experienced in discovering the depths of the eucharistic mystery.

In this first chapter, I follow Pope John Paul's example and return to the Upper Room where the Last Supper occurred. I picture the setting and the order of service for the first Eucharist. I draw this

The Exodus Passover

The Passover described in Exodus 12:1–14, 21–28 is a major scriptural source for understanding the context in which Jesus instituted the Eucharist. When a father blessed the unleavened bread, he evoked memories of first Passover when the bread was eaten in haste. The family would also recall the manna in the desert and acknowledge that they live by the bread of God's Word. When they drank the Cup of Blessing at the end of the meal, they experienced festive joy as they thought about the promise of a future messiah. They could also picture Melchizedek's sacrifice of bread and wine that was an image of their own offering. Finally, the presence of the holy lamb, sanctified at the temple, made present their own desire to offer themselves to God. Lastly, the Hallel psalms (113 through 118) are Passover hymns designated for this celebration.

material from Scripture and the pope's inspiring reflections as well as various descriptions of Passover meals.

While there has been a longstanding debate as to whether the Last Supper was a Passover meal, there is no doubt that the early Christians viewed it from the perspective of Passover. From the Passover meal, I have preserved the essentials and, from differing accounts, retained details that seemed best suited to open our hearts to the wondrous mystery of the institution of the Eucharist.

JESUS WITNESSES HUMBLE SERVICE

Soon after his triumphal entry into Jerusalem, Jesus instructed his disciples to prepare for their Passover meal. They selected an upper room. Most houses at the time were one-storey homes. Many of them had a small room on the roof and it served as an attic for storage. However, some of the larger homes contained a spacious room on the roof that was used by rabbis for meetings to study Scripture and pastoral issues. An outside stairway led to the upper room, also called the *cenacle*—a term derived from the Latin and meaning "a dining room." It was in such a place that the Lord's Supper occurred.

For such an important gathering, the apostles would have bathed. But their sandaled bare feet would get dirty walking through unpaved, dusty—and sometimes muddy—streets. At the door of the dining room, they would expect a servant, ready to wash their feet with a pitcher of water, a bowl and a towel.

That evening they were dismayed and puzzled to find Jesus greeting them in a servant's humble role. Their master and teacher would wash their feet. Jesus prepared them for the Eucharist by giving them the example of humility. Saint Paul wrote to the Philippians (2:5–11) that Jesus, beginning his journey of humility, had emptied himself of the status of divine glory and taken on the role of a slave totally obedient to the Father. Scripture scholars call this process the emptying (*kenosis* in Greek). As Jesus knelt before the apostles, he reached another level of the emptying, the humility he wanted to teach them.

Believing this was unworthy of Christ, Peter resisted being washed. "You will never wash my feet" (John 13:8a). Jesus insisted that this was necessary; otherwise, Peter would have no participation in Christ's life, the Eucharist or the church. "Unless I wash you, you have no share with me" (John 13:8b). Peter replied that Jesus should wash not only his feet, but his hands and head as well. Knowing that Peter had already bathed, Jesus said that washing his feet would be sufficient to drive home the point of the call to humble service.

> Do you know what I have done to you? You call me Teacher and Lord—and you are right, for that is what I am. So if I, your Lord and Teacher, have washed your feet, you also ought to wash one another's feet. For I have set you an example, that you also should do as I have done to you. (John 13:12–14)

Jesus showed them and us that an attitude of humble service is the best way to prepare for the celebration of Eucharist. Humility opens us to the love Christ wishes to give us. Humility invites us to the privilege of serving others.

THE SETTING FOR THE LAST SUPPER

What did the apostles see as they entered the dining room? They saw a short-legged table close to the floor. It was surrounded by cushions

The Last Supper, by Duccio, offers a view of the Upper Room with the disciples seated on cushions around the table. This arrangement would have been more typical than the Renaissance portrayal of Leonardo da Vinci's Last Supper.

on which they would sit. On the table was a bowl of saltwater to remind them of the tears that were shed during the time slavery of their ancestors in Egypt. Another bowl contained bitter-tasting salads that evoked the feelings of resentment and helplessness against the iron rule of the pharaoh. The participants would dip the salad into the saltwater before eating it.

Nearby rested large platters of unleavened bread, recalling the haste to leave Egypt. Leavened bread would have consumed too much time to prepare. Next to the bread were bowls of dip made of crushed apples, dates and nuts, sprinkled with cinnamon to remind them of the bricks they made in the slave times.

At the center of the table was a roast lamb. The day before, two apostles had gone to the temple, purchased a lamb and gave it to the priest for a sacrificial offering. After slaying the lamb, the priest poured out its blood—symbol of life—on the altar of sacrifice and so conse-crated the lamb to God. The priest then took a small portion of it and put it in the fire as a holocaust. Removed from human use, it now belonged to God as a sacrifice. Symbolically it went to God's "table."

Made holy by this ritual, the remainder of the lamb was given to the apostles for their Passover meal. Now in the middle of their table was this lamb that symbolized sacrifice. Of course, Jesus would be the real Lamb of God about to be sacrificed the next day.

Finally, there were three cups of wine mixed with some water before each of the participants' places and one large Cup of Blessing filled with wine. The wine signified the gladdening of the human heart when the gift of freedom was received. Instructed since they were chil-dren by their parents in the symbolism of the Passover meal, the expe-rienced participants at this supper could immediately read the mean-ing of these foods:

- saltwater
- bitter salad dip
- unleavened bread
- lamb
- three cups of wine at each place
- Cup of Blessing

THE ORDER OF SERVICE

To gain a sense of the progress of the events of the Lord's Supper, I have divided them into seven parts:

1. The Toast
2. Jesus Changes the Bread Into His Body
3. The Supper of the Lamb
4. The Cup of Blessing
5. Do This in Memory of Me
6. Jesus Sings
7. The Fourth Cup

In trying to reconstruct these scenes, I hope I have been able to preserve a sense of the divine mystery of faith that is being described. I believe we need to see these scenes as if for the first time. This requires of us a feeling of wonder and even of radical amazement at the remarkable gift that Jesus gave us that night long ago. Ultimately, we are called to have faith in the truth of the Eucharist.

1. The Toast

Just as it is customary with many of us on special occasions to raise a glass of wine or water or fruit juice at the start of a meal with a toast to each other's health, so also the Passover supper began with a toast to God. Jesus and his apostles raised the first cup of wine and praised God for the gifts of creation, salvation and continuing providence.

> Praise the LORD!
> How good it is to sing praises to our God;
>> for he is gracious, and a song of praise is fitting.
>
> …
>
> He heals the brokenhearted,
>> and binds up their wounds.
>
> …
>
> Great is our Lord, and abundant in power;
>> his understanding is beyond measure.
>
> …
>
> Sing to the LORD with thanksgiving;
>> make melody to our God on the lyre.
> (Psalm 147:1, 3, 5, 7)

If this had been a family Passover, the youngest son would ask, "Why is this night more important than any other night?" Usually, the father would then recite a summary of the story of Israel's delivery from Egypt. Since the Lord's Supper was not a family setting, perhaps an apostle asked the question and the group possibly would have sung Psalm 136. Jesus would sing each verse that detailed the freedom story and the rest would respond, "For his mercy endures forever." The following verses illustrate what that would be like:

O give thanks to the LORD, for he is good,
    for his steadfast love endures forever;
...
who struck Egypt through their firstborn,
    for his steadfast love endures forever;
and brought out Israel from among them,
    for his steadfast love endures forever;
who divided the Red Sea in two,
    for his steadfast love endures forever;
and made Israel pass through the midst
    of it,
    for his steadfast love endures forever;
(Psalm 136:1, 10–11, 13–14)

This remembering of the mighty saving deeds of God would become a model for the Eucharist in which we remember Christ's salvation acts now present for us by the power of the Holy Spirit through the ministry of the priest.

Then Jesus said, "I have eagerly desired to eat this Passover with you before I suffer" (Luke 22:15). We can gather from John's Gospel, chapters 13—17, what thoughts Jesus planted in their hearts that night. He called them friends, not servants, and branches that would live from him, the vine. He prayed to the Father to protect them. He promised to send them the Holy Spirit who would remind them of his teachings and

The Words of Institution

The words of the institution of the Eucharist are found in Matthew 26:26–28, Mark 14:22–24, Luke 22:17, 19–20 and 1 Corinthians 11:23–25. The texts vary in their details. The Eucharist had already been celebrated for over a generation before the writing of these accounts and slight variations occurred depending on the emphasis desired by a given community. Of course, the full narrative of the Lord's Supper as it appears in each scriptural account should be read to appreciate the context of the institution of the Eucharist.

Gradually, the church created a uniform text that is faithful to Christ's words in Scripture. However, we need to remember that these words belong in a broader context that includes the Liturgy of the Word and the Eucharistic Prayer of which six forms are presently used. We will spend more time on this fact in future chapters.

What has happened? For almost two thousand years men have prayed and probed and fought over the meaning of these words.... When Jesus spoke and acted as he did, he knew that all he said and did was of divine importance. He wished to be understood, and spoke accordingly. The disciples were no symbolists, neither were they nineteenth- or twentieth-century conceptualists, but simple fishermen much more inclined to take Jesus' words literally—if not with crude realism, as they had at Capharnaum—than spiritually.
—*Romano Guardini*

help them to understand and witness them.

2. Jesus Changes the Bread Into His Body

Next came the ritual of the taking, blessing, breaking and distribution of the bread. The ceremony of the bread symbolized their bond of love with each other since they all partook of the one bread. Jesus took one of the large pieces of bread and blessed it. We have an echo of the substance of his blessing in the offering of the bread at our Masses:

> Blessed are you, Lord God of all creation. Through your goodness we have this bread to offer, which earth has given and human hands have made. It will become for us the bread of life.

After the traditional blessing prayer Jesus added new words, "Take and eat; this is my body, given up for you." Then he broke the bread, changed into his body, and gave it to each of them.

It was not customary to change the essentials of the ceremony. But Jesus did this when he changed the bread into his body. His words were clear. None of the texts of institution describes what went on in the minds and hearts of the disciples. Pope John Paul II wondered about their reaction:

> Did the apostles who took part in the Last Supper understand the meaning of the words spoken by Christ? Perhaps

not. Those words would only be fully clear at the end of the *Triduum sacrum*, the time from Thursday evening to Sunday morning.[1] They had heard Christ's eucharistic teaching given at Capernaum and recorded in John. It is likely that he reviewed and explained this mystery on other occasions as any teacher would. They had witnessed the bread miracles and accepted his teaching on the Bread of Life. Peter spoke for them, "Lord, to whom can we go? You have the words of eternal life" (John 6:68). Now for the first time they received the Body of Christ.

They would not have missed Jesus' alarming statement that his body "will be given up for you." The expression had a sacrificial meaning. He told them he would die for them. The Eucharist is a holy meal and it is also a holy sacrifice. The austere words of the Gospel account omit a description of the apostles' thoughts and feelings about the Eucharist that evening. As time unfolded, they would come to know and understand this sacred mystery.

3. The Supper of the Lamb

Next, the main part of the meal took place. They ate bread, dip, salad and lamb, washing it down with the second cup of wine. They dined without benefit of cutlery. Taking a chunk of the unleavened bread in

Bread Miracles

The Gospel accounts of the multiplication of the loaves, the bread miracle, also foreshadow the Eucharist. This miracle is found in all four Gospels and twice in Matthew and Mark:

Matthew 14:13–21 and 15:32–38

Mark 6:33–44 and 8:1–21

Luke 9:10–17

John 6:1–15

This miracle illustrates Christ's human concern for the people's physical hunger and his spiritual desire to meet the needs of their souls. In addition, Jesus takes the bread, blesses it, breaks it and gives it, four steps that foreshadow what he will do in instituting the Eucharist.

John's account of the bread miracle is woven into Christ's dialogue with those who had either heard of the miracle or actually experienced it. His listeners recall the gift of the manna during Israel's years in the desert. Jesus draws them in to hear about his teachings on the Eucharist.

John does not record the words of institution, but he reports Christ's vivid description of the bread becoming his body and the wine his blood. "[F]or my flesh is true food and my blood is true drink. Those who eat my flesh and drink my blood abide in me and I in them" (John 6:55–56).

Furthermore, John devotes chapters 14—17 to Christ's teachings during the Last Supper, singling out themes that tell us how we can apply the mystery of the Eucharist to our lives.

The Breaking of the Bread Narratives

One of the first phrases the early church used for Eucharist was "the breaking of the bread." Luke's Gospel contains such an experience in the touching story of the two disciples on the road to the village of Emmaus (Luke 24:13–35). The risen Jesus meets them and accompanies them on their journey. They do not recognize him until they sit with him at a meal near Emmaus. "When he was at the table with them, he took bread, blessed and

their hands, they used it to feast on the salad and on the other foods, especially enjoying the lamb. While their conversation would normally be festive, a dark mood filled the room after two painful comments by Jesus.

THE BETRAYER

He startled them by saying, "[O]ne of you will betray me, one who is eating with me" (Mark 14:18). Distressed, each apostle asked, "Surely, not I?" (Mark 14:19). Leonardo da Vinci captured this moment in his huge fresco, portraying each apostle in various poses of shock, questioning and dismay, except for Judas pulling back into the shadows while clutching the money bag.

Peter prompted John to ask who the traitor was. Jesus told John that it would be the man who dipped bread into the dish with him. When Judas did this, Jesus said to him, "Do quickly what you are going to do" (John 13:27). Lest we forget what Judas did, our third Eucharistic Prayer introduces the words of institution with the phrase, "On the night he was betrayed...".

PETER'S DENIAL FORETOLD

Then Jesus warned them bluntly that he was in mortal danger and would be dead by the end of the next day. Peter declared he would not let this happen. Jesus prophesied that Peter would deny him three times before the cock crowed twice. Jesus looked at the other disciples and predicted that they, too, would abandon him. Their faith and courage were not yet strong enough to stand with him in his time of need and trial.

> You will all become deserters because of me this night; for it is written,
> "I will strike the shepherd,
>   and the sheep of the flock will be scattered." (Matthew 26:31)

4. The Cup of Blessing

As they completed the main part of the meal, it was time to share in the Cup of Blessing. This was a large chalice of wine from which all would drink. In the human sense, it symbolized their communal friendship with each other. Jesus now gave that ceremony a new meaning. Taking the cup, he blessed it, reciting words similar to the ones we presently use in blessing the cup of wine at our Eucharist:

> Blessed are you, Lord, God of all creation. Through your goodness we have this wine to offer, fruit of the vine and work of human hands. It will become for us our spiritual drink.

Once again, he changed part of the Passover ritual and added new words and a new reality: "Take and drink, this is the cup of my blood, the blood of the new and eternal

broke it, and gave it to them. Then their eyes were opened, and they recognized him" (Luke 24:30–31).

The Catechism of the Catholic Church cites the breaking of bread as one of the names given to Eucharist:

The Breaking of Bread, because Jesus used this rite, part of a Jewish meal...above all at the Last Supper [Cf. Mt 26:26; 1 Cor 11:24]. It is by this action that his disciples will recognize him after his Resurrection [Lk 24:13–35], and it is this expression that the first Christians will use to designate their Eucharistic assemblies [Cf. Acts 2:42, 46; 20:7, 11] (CCC, 1329).

covenant. It will be shed for you for the forgiveness of sins." Here I often think of the wine miracle that Jesus performed at the marriage feast at Cana as an act of kindness to relieve the embarrassed couple from the awkward news that the wine supply had run out. It was also a prophetic sign of what Jesus would do at the Last Supper when he changed wine into his blood. An early church Father wrote a hymn that connected Cana with Christ's changing wine into his blood.

> When Christ clearly changed the water into wine through his own power, the whole world was filled with cheer, finding the taste of that wine most agreeable. Today we can sit at the banquet of the church, because the wine has changed into the blood of Christ, and we drink it in holy joy, glorifying the Great Spouse.[2]

The Tassilo Chalice, circa 770 AD.

When he had changed the bread into his body, he told his apostles it would be given up in death for them. He repeated this truth when he changed the wine into his blood, telling them it would be shed to bring them salvation from sin. The Supper of the Lord turned out to be a holy meal and a holy sacrifice. Saint Paul taught the Corinthians the same truth, "For as often as you eat this bread and drink the cup, you proclaim the Lord's death until he comes" (1 Corinthians 11:26).

Further, Jesus said that the wine become his blood would initiate a new covenant between God and his people, a relationship of eternal love. The covenant with Israel that God made through Moses on Mount Sinai prepared the way for this new and permanent covenant that Jesus instituted in the Upper Room. As the Cup of Blessing passed into the hands of each apostle and they drank, they experienced a new and profound bonding with Jesus and one another. Saint Paul explained it well:

The cup of blessing that we bless, is it not a sharing in the blood of Christ? The bread that we break, is it not a sharing in the body of Christ? Because there is one bread, we who are many are one body, for we all partake of the one bread. (1 Corinthians 10:16–17)

Therefore, Jesus chose bread and wine to be the sacraments of his body and blood because they are examples of a process of unification and reconciliation achieved through Christ's death and resurrection. The one bread is made from many grains of wheat and the one cup of wine results from many grapes. So also, many people are brought to unity through Christ's body and blood.

The wheat and the grapes undergo processes of pain and renewal. The wheat seeds die in the earth beneath and then rise as stalks of wheat only to be ground by millstones to become flour and finally are baked with fire to become bread. Grapes are crushed in the winepress on their way to becoming wine. Jesus applied these images to our spiritual transformation: "Very truly, I tell you, unless a grain of wheat into the earth and dies, it remains just a single grain; but if it dies, it bears much fruit" (John 12:24).

When we eat bread and drink wine, we change these elements into ourselves, but when we consume the eucharistic Body and Blood of Christ, we are changed into Christ. Through our lifelong Holy Communions, Jesus gradually strengthens our faith, perfects our love and gives us the courage to witness him without fear in this world. We pray:

O Jesus, joy of loving hearts, the fount of life and my true light,
I seek the peace your love imparts, and stand rejoicing in your sight.
I taste in you my living bread and long to feast upon you still.
I drink of you my fountainhead, my thirsting soul to quench and fill.
O Jesus ever with me stay; make all my moments calm and bright.
O chase the night of sin away; shed o'er the world your holy light.[3]

5. Do This in Memory of Me

Once Jesus instituted the Eucharist, he said to his apostles, "Do this in remembrance of me" (Luke 22:19). By this command, Jesus conveyed to them the priestly power of celebrating the Eucharist. He formed them into an ordained priesthood, a sacramental power that they would pass on to bishops who in turn would do the same for priests. Pope John Paul II wrote eloquently of the importance of these words of Christ.

> When he says to the apostles: "Do this in remembrance of me!" he constitutes *the ministers of this sacrament* in the church, in which for all time the sacrifice offered by him for the redemption of the world must continue.... Holy Thursday is every year *the day of the birth of the Eucharist* and *the birthday of our priesthood.*[4]

Jesus commissioned the apostles to celebrate the Eucharist as a memorial of his saving life, passion, death and resurrection. As a sacrament, the Eucharist on Holy Thursday night looked forward to the salvation events about to happen. As a sacrament, the Eucharist after the resurrection on Easter Sunday would remember, that is, make present the salvation accomplished for us by Christ.

When we use the term "remember," we recall past events, but they remain so. The discovery of America happens only once. We can read the stories of George Washington, Benjamin Franklin, Abraham Lincoln, Harriet Beecher Stowe and other national heroes. They live in our memories as past figures, though their lives and teachings still inspire and inform us.

However, in Scripture the divine order of history gives a different meaning to memory. For the Jewish people, their Passover made present their historical liberation from Egypt and celebrated God's continuing providence in their lives. For the Christian people, the Holy Eucharist makes present to us Christ's redemption and celebrates the gift of divine life. Humanly speaking, memory can be a recall of past events that are not present now. Divinely speaking, by the power of the Holy Spirit, through our memory Christ's saving acts are made present now in the Eucharist. Our faith recognizes this and helps us benefit from the graces offered to us. We can grow in a stronger faith in this mystery by repeating the prayer of the desperate father imploring Jesus to help his son, "I believe; help my unbelief" (Mark 9:24).

6. Jesus Sings

In our hasty culture, we seldom linger at the table as our meal comes to a close. Yet in earlier times, the pleasure of table fellowship was more common. Jesus and the apostles had completed their meal and finished what had become the first eucharistic celebration. There was joy at the Lord's Supper indicated by a detail: Jesus sang a hymn of praise with the apostles, the only time Scripture reports him as singing. "When they had sung the hymn, they went out to the Mount of Olives" (Matthew 26:30).

In reality, he would often have sung the psalms both at synagogue and temple services, yet only in the solemn and somewhat brooding atmosphere of the Upper Room does a Gospel writer remember him singing. It was customary to sing one or two psalms from the "Praise Collection," numbers 113–118, also referred to as the Hallel or alleluia psalms, a term that means "Praise God." Following is a sample of a psalm Jesus could have used:

What shall I return to the LORD
   for all his bounty to me?
I will lift up the cup of salvation
   and call on the name of the LORD,

. . .

I will offer to you a thanksgiving sacrifice
   and call on the name of the LORD.

. . .

in the courts of the house of the LORD,
   in your midst, O Jerusalem.
(Psalm 116:12–13, 17, 19)

THE LEGEND OF THE THORN BIRD

This psalm reminds me of the legend of the song of the thorn bird. After it leaves the nest and embarks on its life, it searches for a thorn bush that has the longest and sharpest thorns. When its time to die has come, the bird impales itself on such a thorn. Then the bird sings its final song that outcarols the lark and the nightingale and even invites God to stop and listen. The lesson of the legend is that the greatest work of beauty is purchased only at the price of ultimate sacrifice. Jesus did not sing for his supper; he sang for our supper—the Eucharist that brings us the salvation he achieved in his passion, death and resurrection.

Jesus is about to walk to Gethsemane, yet he sings. Saint Augustine often was fascinated by music, especially the songs of the farmers at harvest time. In his reflections on the psalms, he writes of the power of a song to represent love:

> A song is a thing of joy; more profoundly it is a thing of love. Anyone, therefore, who has learned to love the new life has learned to sing a new song.... Look, you tell me, I am singing. Yes indeed, you are singing; you are singing clearly, I can hear you.... Sing with your voices, your hearts, your lips and your lives.[5]

Jesus certainly sang that night with love and with the resolve to lay down his life for our salvation.

7. The Fourth Cup

Some believe the customary fourth cup of wine was not drunk that evening since this is not clear from Scripture. Dr. Scott Hahn suggests that Jesus was offered the "fourth" cup of wine at the last moment of his life on the cross. It coincided with his having fulfilled all that he was called to do for us. He drank this cup of wine that signified the complete acceptance of the suffering he endured to save us from sin and bring us a participation in divine life.

In John's Gospel account of Christ on the cross, Jesus said that he was thirsty. When the soldier offered him wine, he drank it. In a way this was the fourth cup he had not drunk at the table of the Last Supper. Throughout his ministry, Jesus had used the image of drinking the cup to describe his commitment to the cross that was essential to his plan to save us. Telling Peter to sheathe his sword in Gethsemane, Jesus said, "Am I not to drink the cup the Father has given me?" (John 18:11). According to the other evangelists, at Gethsemane Jesus asked the Father if it were still possible to avoid drinking the cup.

Nevertheless in that garden prayer Jesus resolved to do his Father's will. He followed this act with the words, "It is finished" (John 19:30).

The Hebrew word for this is *kalah*. It is three o'clock in the afternoon. Over at the temple, the priest has just sacrificed the last lamb of Passover and he pronounces the liturgical prayer, kalah. Jesus, the true Lamb of God, has drunk the fourth cup of suffering and pronounced the completion and perfection of all the sacrifices that foreshadowed his own.

From now on, the sacrament of the Eucharist will make Christ's sacrifice present for salvation and the gift of divine life to all who participate in this celebration.

I only want to say
If there is a way
Take this cup away from me
for I don't want to taste
its poison.
—Jesus Christ Superstar

From age to age you gather
a people to yourself,
so that from east to west
a perfect offering may be
made to the glory of your
name.
—Eucharistic Prayer III

Profile

THE LEGEND OF MARCELINO OF THE BREAD AND WINE

Spanish monks of the Middle Ages loved to tell the story of Marcelino Pan y Vino, "Marcelino of the Bread and Wine." Left abandoned by the door of a monastery as a baby, Marcelino (so named because he arrived on the feast of Saint Marcellus) proved to be a ray of sunshine amid the gray stones and black robes of the monks. He grew into a lively little boy who specialized in mischief: a goat's tail tied to the abbey bell, lizards in the salad, a frog in the cook's bed. Friar Cook corrected the boy and said threateningly, "See that stairway. Never go up there. The Big Man will get you."

Naturally, one day Marcelino had to go up the stairs and see who this Big Man was. He found him in that dark attic. He saw the Big Man on a cross. The Big Man had thorns on his head and nails in his hands and pain on his face. At first Marcelino was scared; then he said, "You look hungry." That night he stole bread and wine from the kitchen and brought it to the Big Man. A light appeared in the Big Man's right hand and he reached out and took the food and drink, smiling. After that, Marcelino took good care of the Big Man. When it stormed, Marcelino brought him blankets to comfort him.

One day the Big Man came off the cross, sat down and took Marcelino in his arms. "What would you like most in all the world?" the Big Man asked Marcelino. "To see my mother," said the boy. "Then you must go into a deep sleep. Go to sleep, Marcelino." The next day the monks looked in vain for the child. The cook thought, "He might be upstairs." He and other monks went up the stairs. Slowly they opened the door. The room was flooded with light. Their beloved boy had gone home to see his mother.

This legend conveys to us the truth of the Eucharist. For Marcelino, the bread and wine were his way of saying to Christ, "I love you. I want to take care of you." For us the bread and wine become the body and blood of Jesus is his way of saying, "I love you. I want to take care of you."

Just as the boy asked the Big Man no questions, but set out to serve him because he needed something, so Jesus asks us no questions. He comes to love and serve us. The only thing the boy really hoped for was that the Big Man would open his hand and accept the bread and wine of love. The main thing Jesus asks of us is to open our hands and accept the love he never ceases to offer us.

Jesus wants to take good care of us. His body is food for our bodies; his blood is drink for our souls. Jesus makes it possible to stay in touch with God and to have a life worth living on earth. All we need to do is open our hearts and hands and accept his body and blood.

In return, he asks us to look around and see the needs of others. Those who have all their material needs met are still hungry for God. They thirst for faith and a self-image that is worth loving. Those who lack material goods yearn for bread to stave off starvation and hope for education, health and a decent way of life for their children and families.

Our responsibility as eucharistic persons is to offer others the vision of Jesus Christ, help in their material needs and hope for a better life. Too many have full stomachs and empty souls. Too many have full souls but empty stomachs. To the former, let us bring the good works of faith; to the latter, let us bring the faith that expresses itself in good works.

This is the bread and wine—Christ's body and blood—that we have to offer the world. Just as the Big Man was not so great a problem that he frightened Marcelino, so neither should the big problems of the world make us afraid. Love all the hungry—those who starve for God and those who need bread—and feed them.

PRAYER

Eucharistic Lord, we thank you for the gift of Holy Communion, knowing thereby we are deeply in touch with your love and care. May we then turn to others in the world and minister to their spiritual and physical hungers. Let us be persons of the Eucharist, ready to feed those in need. Because you are our bread of life, we believe we can bring you to all who need you. Amen.

FOR DISCUSSION

1. What details of the Last Supper show us that the Eucharist is both a sacred meal and a sacred sacrifice?

2. How had Jesus prepared the apostles to understand these words at the Last Supper: "Take, eat; this is my body," and "Drink from it, all of you; for this is my blood"?

3. When Jesus said that his body was "given" for us, and that his blood "is poured out" for us, what was he emphasizing? Why is that important for us?

4. Why did Matthew, Mark, Luke and John include Christ's bread miracle in their Gospels?

5. How does the miracle at Cana relate to the mystery of the Eucharist?

6. From this presentation of the setting and order of service at the Last Supper, what helps you to revere the Mass today and your relationship with Christ in Holy Communion?

7. How can you help others to appreciate the truth of the Eucharist? What can you do to increase your faith in the Eucharist and your deeper participation in the Mass?

chapter two

- - - - - - - - - - -

THE
EUCHARIST
IN THE
EARLY
CHURCH

From Apostolic Times to the
Middle of the Third Century

> On Holy Thursday we walk with
> Jesus to the Cross. On Corpus
> Christi we walk with Jesus to the
> Resurrection.
>
> —POPE BENEDICT XVI

In apostolic times, the Upper Room was the shrine where the Eucharist was born on Holy Thursday and the church was born at Pentecost. Jesus had commissioned the apostles to continue celebrating the Eucharist. After receiving the Holy Spirit, they were faced with the question of how to respond to Christ's call. Their Jewish faith and forms of prayer centered on the temple. Synagogue and Sabbath meals influenced the way they would celebrate Eucharist.

THE MEAL

In the beginning the setting of a meal was foremost, since the Eucharist began at a Passover meal. Simply repeating this supper with the addition of Christ's words of institution was not feasible because it was designed to be held only once a year—and only in Jerusalem.

In terms of our culture that would be similar to celebrating Thanksgiving (with turkey and trimmings and the whole family gathered from all over) every Thursday, obviously something neither practical nor desirable. Guided by the Holy Spirit they realized that this celebration should be held on a weekly basis.

Early Christians had another model to draw from: the Jewish family meal on the eve of the weekly Sabbath. This meal normally began with a prayer of praise over the bread at the beginning of the meal and another one over the wine at the end. It concluded with this dialogue:

Host: Let us praise the Lord.
All: The name of the Lord be praised now and forever!
Host: Praised be our God because we eat of his gifts and live by his favor.
All: Praised be he and praised be his name.

The host followed this exchange with praise of God the creator who is faithful to the covenant by giving them their land and dwelling among them. Very likely, the apostles adapted these praise prayers for the bread and wine to apply to the Eucharist and linked them to the words of institution.

The New Testament references to the "breaking of the bread" in Luke 24:13–25 and Acts 2:42, 46 and 20:7, 11 as well as to the "Supper of the Lord" in 1 Corinthians 10:14–17 and 11:17–34 persuade us that the apostles adopted a meal setting for Eucharist. Pope John Paul II confirmed the link between the "breaking of the bread" passages and the Eucharist:

The "breaking of the bread"—as the Eucharist was called in earliest times—has always been at the centre of the Church's life....The account of the Risen Jesus appearing to the two disciples on the road to Emmaus helps us to focus on a primary aspect of the Eucharistic mystery...: *The Eucharist is a mystery of light!*...When the disciples on the way to Emmaus asked Jesus to stay "with" them, he responded by giving them a much greater gift: through the Sacrament of the Eucharist he found a way to stay "in" them.[6]

As the years passed, the apostles and their successors began to separate the Eucharist part of the assembly from the meal. The two texts of institution were brought together as they are seen in the Gospels. Saint Paul notes that the Corinthians met to eat at their own tables apart from Eucharist. The custom of dining before Eucharist was accepted at first, but the emergence of cliques eating with each other, of the rich not sharing their food with the poor and the existence of drunkenness was a scandal that led church leaders to remove the Eucharist from the setting of a meal.

> When you come together, it is not really to eat the Lord's supper. For when the time comes to eat, each of you goes ahead with your own supper, and one goes hungry and another becomes drunk. What! Do you not have homes to eat and drink in?...If you are hungry, eat at home, so that when you come together, it will not be for your condemnation. (1 Corinthians 11:20–21, 34)

Removing the Eucharist from the meal setting also had the advantage of focusing the celebration on the original intent of what happened on Holy Thursday. That evening Jesus did not simply say, "This is my body" and "This is my blood." He added, "which is given for you" and "which is poured out for you." He explained the sacrificial meaning of what he offered them to eat and drink. The Eucharist was a sacrament that made present his sacrifice that would be offered for everyone's salvation. The *Catechism of the Catholic Church* teaches: "The Mass is at the same time, and inseparably, the sacrificial memorial in which the sacrifice of the cross is perpetuated and [is] the sacred banquet of communion with the Lord's body and blood" (*CCC*, 1382).

The ominous mood on Holy Thursday night indicated by Christ's prophecies about the betrayal of Judas, the denial of Peter and the scattering of the apostles because the shepherd would be struck might have caused the apostles to connect the Eucharist with suffering and death. The sorrowful mysteries soon to be lived out by Jesus would teach them what "given" for you and "poured out for you" actually meant. In the weeks and years ahead, they would relive the mystery of the Passion of Christ at each Eucharist. Saint Paul put it succinctly for them, "For as often as you eat this bread and drink the cup, you proclaim the Lord's death until he comes" (1 Corinthians 11:26).

On the other hand, the joyful exultation in the mystery was also relived in the celebration of Eucharist. The sacrament made present both Christ's death and resurrection. The Risen Christ becomes indeed the living bread of life.

At eucharistic gatherings, the apostles and disciples would speak of this as the paschal mystery. Just as the Passover lamb must die before it is eaten, so the Lamb of God must die before rising to new life and becoming the Communion feast for our souls. It is a mystery because it is a work of God that can only be perceived and accepted by faith. It is called "paschal" because Christ embraced a death and resurrection in order for salvation to happen. Saint Paul preached this to the early church. "For our paschal lamb, Christ, has been sacrificed" (1 Corinthians 5:7).

SUNDAY, THE LORD'S DAY

Once the Eucharist was separated from the meal, it was judged that the celebration no longer needed to be held at night, nor on the Jewish Sabbath (Saturday). Very early, the apostles had decided that the Christian Sabbath would be Sunday, the day of the Lord's resurrection and the weekly remembrance of God's creation of the world. The Easter narratives start just before dawn on Sunday. "Early on the first day of the week, while it was still dark, Mary Magdalene came to the tomb and saw that the stone had been removed from the tomb" (John 20:1). With this in mind, the custom developed of having Eucharist early on Sunday morning.

Sunday was filled with special memories of Easter and Pentecost.

Sunday invited early Christians to live again the experience of the two disciples who walked with the Risen Christ on the road to Emmaus, where their hearts burned with love and their eyes beheld their Lord in the breaking of the bread. On the night of Easter Sunday itself, Jesus appeared to the apostles and gave them the gift of the Holy Spirit and the power to forgive sins. "Receive the Holy Spirit. If you forgive the sins of any, they are forgiven them; if you retain the sins of any, they are retained" (John 20:22–23).

On the following Sunday Jesus appeared again to the apostles, including Thomas, to whom Jesus made himself known by showing him the signs of his Passion. Fifty days after the Resurrection, on Pentecost Sunday, the Holy Spirit was given to 120 disciples. This marked the formal beginning of the church.

The leaders of the church called Sunday the Lord's Day because on it Jesus rose from the dead, an event upon which Christian faith is founded. Seen with faith, the resurrected Jesus was historically witnessed by more than five hundred people (cf. 1 Corinthians 15:5–6). From apostolic times, Sunday has been honored as the Lord's Day and the new Sabbath. It was common practice by the time the book of Revelation was written (around the year 90). John testified, "I was in the spirit on the Lord's day, and I heard behind me a loud voice like a trumpet…" (Revelation 1:10).

The Risen Christ and the Holy Spirit had consecrated Sunday by events that formed the faith of the church forever and led the early Christians to hallow Sunday as the Lord's Day on which they would always thereafter celebrate the Eucharist. Besides the evidence of Scripture, we have an interesting reference by a Roman writer about the Christians' worship. Father Joseph Jungmann tells us:

> When about 111–113 A.D., Pliny the Younger, Legate of Bithynia, had arrested and examined a number of Christians, he established the fact that they were in the habit of meeting on a certain fixed day before dawn…and of singing in alternate verses a song to Christ their God.[7]

In pondering this development of the eucharistic celebration, we need to recall the truth of faith that the Eucharist causes the growth of the church. The development is not simply a rational common-sense action, though some of that is present. How does the church grow? What causes the interior insights that expanded the vision of the faith of the apostles—and enlightens our own as well? It is produced by the power of God.

The core source of this divine energy is in the Holy Eucharist. The apostles were doing more than merely arranging ceremonies and rituals; they were experiencing the mystery of light that flowed from their contact with the Eucharist. The cumulative impact of consistent encounter with the graces of the death and resurrection of Christ in this holy sacrament brought them the effects of redemption.

The whole Christian community of their time also was profoundly affected by being fed with the Eucharist. The unifying power of the Eucharist made them strong in mind, heart and soul. The Body of Christ in the Eucharist built them up into the body of Christ as church. "Because there is one bread, we who are many are one body, for we all partake of the one bread" (1 Corinthians 10:17).

The creative imagination of the early church of this period was stirred by the divine food and drink that was itself the origin of creativity. In the Upper Room, the apostles accepted Christ's invitation to enter for the first time into sacramental communion with him. That primordial moment marked the beginning of the process by which the church is built up into the body of Christ until the end of the age. Whatever we say about the history of how the Mass grew and flourished is connected to the nourishment that emanates from the Body and Blood of Christ in the holy sacrament.

THE SYNAGOGUE LITURGY

Now that the Eucharist was separated from the context of a meal, the question arose as to what would replace the supper. More would be needed than the words of institution. Since most of the first Christians were Jewish, they already had the experience of synagogue worship to work with. Luke's description of Christ's first sermon in the synagogue at Nazareth gives us an idea of what would occur (see Luke 4:14–30).

A synagogue was a simple meeting room designed for prayer and religious teaching. People sat around a platform on which were a table, some chairs and a lectern. In the wall behind this was an enclosure usually covered with a veil of precious cloth. Inside was a copy of the scrolls of Scripture, especially the Torah (the first five books of the Bible) and the Prophets. The men sat on benches and the women looked on from a space behind wooden latticework. Generally, the building was modest in size.

The synagogue was managed by an administrator or president. The reader of Scripture and giver of the sermon need

Ruins of an ancient synagogue at Capernaum, in Israel.

not be a rabbi or other professionally trained religious leader. Guests could be invited to perform this task, which was what occurred to Jesus that day. After a prayer, the administrator handed Jesus a scroll that contained chapter sixty-one of the book of Isaiah. Jesus unrolled the scroll and read the passage in Hebrew.

He then recited the passage again, this time in Aramaic, since many people did not understand classical Hebrew. Jesus rolled up the document and gave it back to the president. He proceeded to give a homily on the text about the coming Messiah and applied the words to himself. His words provoked anger and the assembly broke up. In less controversial circumstances, his talk might have stimulated a moderate discussion with some life applications. The service would have ended with a closing prayer.

The structure is clear: prayer, reading of Scripture, sermon, discussion and closing prayer. Nothing in this scene mentions singing the psalms or having several readings, though that may have been customary at special times. Saint Paul, during his mission journeys, took advantage of the custom of having guest preachers in synagogues to give his talks on Christ and appeal for converts.

The leaders of the early church adapted this model of synagogue liturgy to the Eucharist, becoming in effect a liturgy of the Word that led up to the prayers of blessings, thanksgiving and words of institution. What texts were read? We can only imagine exactly what they did, but there are reasonable inferences we can make. Until the early 50s, when Saint Paul's letters began to be circulated, the only available Scriptures were from the Old Testament. They could read from the Prophets, especially those passages dealing with the Messiah. They could also choose texts concerned with the covenant and apply them to the new covenant with Christ.

They would have chosen the creation narratives that included the creation of Adam and Eve and their life in paradise followed by the temptation and fall and the promise of a redeemer that could be employed for their obvious application to the salvation Christ accomplished for them.

At the same time, the apostles' and disciples' memories of Christ's words and deeds eventually fixed in oral tradition would have been part of the celebration. In an oral culture, memories were strong, cultivated and admired. By the year 80, the Gospels of Mark, Matthew and Luke and all the letters of Paul were written and would be used. John's Gospel would have been available by the year 90.

DIDACHE

Beside the development of the liturgy of the Word influenced by the synagogue ritual, there was also a growth of prayer surrounding the words of institution. It became know as the prayer of thanksgiving, or the Eucharistic Prayer. We have an example of this from the *Didache*, or the "Teaching of the Apostles," a document written some time around the year 60. Chapters nine and ten of the *Didache* provide prayers to be used for "thanksgiving" (the Eucharist):

> With regard to the prayer of thanksgiving *(eucharistia)*, offer it in this fashion. First, for the cup: "We thank you, our Father, for the holy vine of David, your servant....Glory be yours through all ages! Amen." Then for the bread broken: "We thank you, our Father, for the life and knowledge you have revealed to us through Jesus your servant. Glory be yours through all ages! Amen. Just as the bread broken was first scattered on the hills, then gathered and became one, so let your church be gathered from the ends of the earth into your kingdom, for yours is glory and power through all ages! Amen.[8]

By the year 150, the general structure of the eucharistic liturgy had been established. In its fundamental structure, it remains the same to the present time. As we watch its progress through history, we will see a number of accidental additions and subtractions, but what we have now is substantially what a mid–second century Christian would have experienced.

There will be language changes, variations in the way people participated in the Mass, undue expansions—even intrusions—of

Come together on the Lord's day, break bread and give thanks, having first confessed your sins so that your sacrifice may be pure. Anyone who has a quarrel with his fellow Christian should not gather with you until the two are reconciled....

—Didache

Readings and Homily

[O]n the day named after the sun, all who live in the city or countryside assemble, and the memoirs of the apostles or the writings of the prophets are read for as long as time allows. When the lector has finished, the president addresses us, admonishing us and exhorting us to imitate the splendid things we have heard. Then we all stand and pray and...when we have finished praying, bread and wine and water are brought up.

—Justin Martyr

Eucharistic Prayer

Then bread and a cup containing water and wine mixed with water are brought to him who presides over the brethren: he takes them and offers prayer, glorifying the Father of all things through the name of the Son: and he utters a lengthy thanksgiving [Eucharistic Prayer that included the words of institution] because the Father has judged us worthy of these gifts. When the prayer of thanksgiving is ended, the people present give their assent with an "Amen!"

musical performances, proliferations of pageantry and counter movements to pare away these accretions. We will also see the Mass reflecting theological preferences of a given age such as an emphasis on community in Christ followed by a movement to privatization of the Eucharist that echoed the devotion of an age in which the individual relationship with the Eucharist was paramount.

The advantage of this historical journey permits us to have a richer view of our eucharistic practice today and a grateful heart for the recovery of so much that was valuable in New Testament times and the early church.

JUSTIN MARTYR

In the year 150 a convert and philosopher named Justin wrote a description of a Eucharist as it was practiced in the East at Ephesus and in the West at Rome. He wrote this in his *First Apology,* a book defending the faith. He was one of the first Christian writers to make the faith known through published works that countered misconceptions of Christianity by both pagans and Jews. He is known as Justin Martyr since he chose to die by beheading rather than worship the Roman gods.

We learn from Justin that the Mass was held on Sunday as had already become customary in the days of the apostles. The true presence of our Lord Jesus in the bread and wine is clearly stated and assumed since among the believers there was no confusion or denial of this truth of faith. The participation of the community was acknowledged as their assent of "Amen" is mentioned two times. As a key document, this testimony of Justin Martyr provides powerful evidence about the development of the eucharistic liturgy by the middle of the second century and is a substantial landmark in the history of the Mass.

His account tells us that the basic structure of the Mass was already in place throughout the church. Justin wrote that on Sunday there were two readings by a lector, a homily by the priest and the bringing up of the gifts, then the Eucharistic Prayer and the distribution of Communion. And, yes, there was a collection:

> The wealthy who are willing make contributions, each as he pleases, and the collection is deposited with the president who aids orphans and widows, those who are in want because of sickness or other cause...; in short, he takes care of all in need.[9]

HOUSE LITURGIES

We have become so accustomed to churches, chapels, cathedrals, bell towers, spires, stained glass, altars, sculptures,

...[Then] those whom we call "deacons" distribute the bread and wine and water, over which the thanksgiving has been spoken to each of those present; they also carry them to those who were absent.

—Justin Martyr

Real Presence

This food we call "eucharist," and no one may share it unless he believes that our teaching is true.... For we do not receive these things as though they were ordinary food and drink. Just as Jesus Christ our Savior was made flesh through the word of God...for our salvation, so too (we have been taught) through the word of prayer that comes from him, the food over which the thanksgiving [that included the words of institution] has been spoken becomes the flesh and blood of the incarnate Jesus.

—Justin Martyr

The Supper at Emmaus, *by Caravaggio, suggests the sort of table fellowship that would have been prevalent in early house churches.*

organs, choirs and other elements of the place where Mass is celebrated that we tend to forget that for the first three centuries of the
church the Mass usually took place in someone's home. They followed
the example of the early Christian church as expressed in Acts 2:46:
"Day by day, as they spent much time together in the temple, they
broke bread at home."

Here are some other examples of New Testament testimony about
house churches:

Greet Prisca and Aquila, who work with me in Christ Jesus.... Greet
also the church in their house. (Romans 16:3, 5).

The churches of Asia send greetings. Aquila and Prisca, together
with the church in their house, greet you warmly in the Lord.
(1 Corinthians 16:19)

Give my greetings to the brothers and sisters in Laodicea, and to
Nympha and the church in her house. (Colossians 4:15)

[A salutation to] Philemon our dear friend and co-worker,...to

Archippus our fellow soldier, and to the church in your house. (Philemon 1–2).

Chapters two and three of the book of Revelation record John's letters to the seven churches. The term *church* refers to the Christian communities in the seven cities and the houses where they gathered for prayer, Eucharist and mutual encouragement. The Roman state would not tolerate Christian temples or churches—they would not even permit meeting halls that might be the equivalent of the Jewish synagogues. Christians had no choice but to gather in designated homes or house churches. Ordained bishops and presbyters (priests) presided at the liturgies. The anonymity of the worship place protected them from the watchful eye of a hostile government.

Normally the kind of house that was chosen for worship was large enough to accommodate a substantial number of people— some homes of the time could welcome nearly a hundred people in a large hall or atrium. A table was situated at one end of the room. Next to it was a reading stand from which the passages from Scripture would be read. During the celebration the participants stood. We receive from Saint Paul a picture of what it was like from his words to the house churches at Collossae as he invites them to place the words of Christ in their hearts, to continue to be concerned

Difficulties With House Liturgies

Saint Paul's First Letter to the Corinthians 10:14–22 and 11:3–34 treats of discipline (women's head coverings at liturgy) and, more seriously, factions and lack of charity for the community's poorer members by its richer ones. These issues will be treated at greater length in chapter two as we trace the development of eucharistic liturgy after the Last Supper with the growth of house churches.

about each other and to sing praises to God. "Let the word of Christ dwell in you richly; teach and admonish one another in all wisdom; and with gratitude in your hearts sing psalms, hymns, and spiritual songs to God" (Colossians 3:16).

What languages were used for worship? The language for the first Eucharist at the Last Supper was Aramaic. This would be the language for Eucharist among the Jewish Christians of Judea, Galilee, Antioch and probably other parts of the empire. It has remained the language for the liturgies of the Christians of the Chaldean churches in present-day Syria and Iraq. With the arrival of gentile converts, the Eucharist began to be celebrated in Greek and in Latin, but also in Coptic for the Egyptians and the Ethiopians. More will be said about liturgical languages later in this book.

CATACOMBS

Another setting for Eucharist was the catacombs. The catacombs were a network of underground tunnels that became the burial places for Christians during the centuries of persecutions. Niches were dug into

the walls; several bodies were placed in the space and then sealed with a stone slab. In time, the walls were decorated with paintings of biblical scenes and Christian symbols. Catacombs were built in Malta, Sicily, Asia Minor, North Africa and parts of Western Europe, but the most elaborate ones were constructed in Rome. The government did not bother them since the state had laws against molesting tombs.

Catacomb of Saint Callisto in Rome, showing burial niches and an altar.

The most sacred part of the catacombs was the area where the martyrs and other saints were buried. Liturgies were celebrated on the anniversary of a martyr's death. When a larger number of people

began attending the Eucharist, more space was dug out to accommodate them. Eventually, when churches were allowed to be built, the
relics were moved to shrines that honored them.

HIPPOLYTUS

The second Eucharistic Prayer in our liturgy is brief and simple and
owes its inspiration to a similar prayer composed by Hippolytus of
Rome in the year 215. He was a priest and a brilliant theologian who
wrote his books in Greek. Among his writings was a work called *The
Apostolic Tradition*, so named because he believed he was presenting a
faithful vision of the worship of the church of apostolic times. In his
book, he composed a beautiful Eucharistic Prayer that illustrated the
maturity of the Roman liturgy of the third century and was much
admired throughout the rest of the church.

• • •

Eucharistic Prayer by Hippolytus

*Hippolytus's Eucharistic Prayer can be seen as having the following parts:
opening dialogue; thanksgiving for the Incarnation and redemption; the
words of institution; a remembrance and offering; invocation to the Holy
Spirit and doxology. Here is a translation of his text:*

Bishop: "The Lord be with you.
All: And with your spirit.
Bishop: Lift up your hearts.
All: We have lifted them up to the Lord.
Bishop: Let us give thanks to the Lord.
All: It is right and just.

*Bishop: We thank you, O God, through your beloved child Jesus Christ,
whom you have sent to us in the final age as Savior and Redeemer and
messenger of your will;
who is your Word, inseparable from you, through whom you created all
things, and who was pleasing to you;
whom you sent from heaven into the womb of a Virgin and who, having*

been conceived, took flesh and was manifested as your Son, being born of the Holy Spirit and the Virgin;

who carried out your will and won for you a holy people;

who extended his arms in suffering, in order to free from suffering those who trust in you;

who, when he was about to hand himself over to his passion, in order to destroy death and break the devil's chains, to tread hell under foot and lead the just to the light, to fix the term and reveal the resurrection, took bread, gave you thanks, and said, "Take and eat: this is my body which will be broken for you";

who in like manner took the cup and said, "This is my blood that is poured out for you. When you do this, do it in memory of me."

Therefore, remembering his death and resurrection, we offer to you the bread and the cup, and we thank you for deeming us worthy to stand before you and serve you.

We ask you to send your Holy Spirit upon the offering of your holy Church, and to grant that all your saints who share in it may be filled with the Holy Spirit and strengthened in their belief in the truth, so that we may praise and glorify you through your child Jesus Christ, through whom be glory and honor given to you, the Father, and to the Son with the Holy Spirit in your holy Church, now and for all ages.

All: Amen.

Profile

THE EUCHARIST IN A PRISON CELL

In the year 2000 I was in Rome to attend the beatification of Pope John XXIII. I was part of a pilgrimage sponsored by Pope John XXIII Seminary in Weston, Massachusetts, where I was a teacher. On our final evening we had a farewell dinner during which I met one of our guests, an unassuming archbishop who worked at the Vatican. He told me his name was Francis and that he was from Vietnam. Here is his story:

I was a priest in Saigon at the time the Americans were leaving the country and witnessed the turmoil and the fear. Three months later I was appointed the bishop of the diocese. The government wanted me to conform to rules that would impair my ability to serve my people and harm the effectiveness of the church. For example, I would not be permitted to continue the church's services to the needs of the poor. I resisted the pressure of the state and refused to obey what my conscience could not accept.

I was given a prison sentence that lasted thirteen years, nine of which were in solitary confinement. When I lived in solitary, I knew I would continue to love God with all my heart. However, how could I love people? The only people I saw were the guards who checked on me on a rotating basis. I decided I must love them, my enemies. I spoke to them with interest in the lives. "How is your family? How many children do you have? How old are they? Are you in good health?"

In time, I had them tell me their troubles. I listened with sympathy. I prayed for them. After a long time I asked a favor one day. Could I have a piece of wood, some wire, a cake of soap and a knife? A guard gave this to me. I cut the wood into the shape of a cross. I wove the wire into a chain. I sliced the soap in half and hid the cross inside, then returned the knife. (He later wore that cross and chain.)

I let another long period go by and then asked another favor. Would it be possible that each month some of my friends could send me a little wine and bread? My request hung in the silent air for quite a while until one day a little bit of bread and wine was given to me.

From then on, I began to celebrate Eucharist in my cell. I placed a tiny bit of bread and a few drops of wine in my hand. I had no books, no lectionary with the readings, and no sacramentary with the words of the liturgy. Besides, there was virtually no light in my prison home. I knew Eucharistic Prayer II by heart as well as a number of psalms.

I also had devoted each day to reflection on words and deeds of Jesus that I could remember from the Gospels. In celebrating the Eucharist I did not feel alone. I felt the presence of the church as well as Mary, the angels and the saints. Above all, I had the awesome presence of Jesus Christ in the Eucharist both at the Mass and in the tiny particle of his real presence I retained for adoration.

The Eucharist became my bread of life in a tangible way for the remaining years of my imprisonment.

"What is your ministry now?" I asked.

"I am in the office of Justice and Peace."

"What are your duties?"

"I am sent to parts of the world where people hate each other. I know what to do to help them get over that."

His name was Archbishop Francis Xavier Thuan. He was made a cardinal soon after that. Two years later he died.

PRAYER

Lord Jesus, living bread, food of Christian pilgrims, nourish us in our journey through life. May your eucharistic manna be the source of strength as we try to live the call of the kingdom of God. We promise sacrificial love, to be bread that is broken, just as you were. Jesus, bread of pilgrims, abide with us. Amen.

FOR DISCUSSION

1. Read Saint Paul's account of troubles with the meals associated with Eucharist in Corinth (1 Corinthians 11:17–33). If you were their pastor, what would you say? What do you think of Paul's words about taking Eucharist in an unworthy manner?

2. The early Christians moved the Eucharist to Sunday and began to speak of Sunday as the Lord's Day. How can we make our contemporary Sunday more of a Lord's Day than it presently is?

3. Why is it important for us Christians to know that our Liturgy of

the Word at Mass was adapted by the apostles from a synagogue prayer service of the first century?

4. Since there was no written New Testament until the years AD 50–80, how did early Christians bring Jesus into their Liturgy of the Word?

5. Why is it valuable for our understanding of the development of the Eucharistic Prayer to know about documents such as *Didache* 60, Justin Martyr's *First Apology* 150, Hippolytus's work in 215? What do you learn from them?

6. The apostles, the disciples and the leaders that followed them drew their life and creativity from their experience of the mystery of light that flowed from the Eucharist. What does this mean? Why should it be noted? How can this work today?

7. What is your reaction to the fact that the Eucharist was celebrated at house liturgies for over three hundred years in the early church? Why did it happen? What was the value of these domestic settings for worship? What do you think of underground house liturgies in China today because of opposition from the state?

chapter three

• • • • • • • • • • •

THE
EUCHARIST
IN THE
AGE
OF THE
FATHERS

> We cannot live without Sunday.
> —SAID BY THE FORTY-NINE ABITENE
> MARTYRS, 304

Pope Benedict XVI offered these words in a homily at the closing Mass of the National Eucharistic Congress in Bari, Italy, in 2005:

This Eucharistic congress...[is] intended to present Sunday again as a "weekly Easter".... The theme chosen, "We Cannot Live without Sunday," takes us back to the year 304, when Emperor Diocletian prohibited Christians, under pain of death, to possess the Scriptures, to meet on Sunday to celebrate the Eucharist, and to build premises for their assemblies. In Abitene, a small village in what today is Tunis, 49 Christians...were taken by surprise on a Sunday while celebrating the Eucharist.... Arrested, they were taken to Carthage to be interrogated by the proconsul Anulinus....

[A]fter being asked why he violated the emperor's orders...[the leader Emeritus said]..."[W]e cannot live without meeting on Sunday to celebrate the Eucharist.

Why Choose Basilicas?

What building form would be most appropriate for the Church to adopt?... The Church's choice is highly significant, for it chose neither temple nor synagogue nor house as its model, but the basilica, or hall of the king. From the outset, the Church thereby aligned itself with secular authority in an extremely high-profile manner. The basilica was an imposing civic building redolent with the power and glory of the Roman Empire. The type of building previously associated in every town with the dispensation of law and order now became synonymous with Christian assembly.

—Richard Giles

We would not have the strength to face the daily difficulties...." After atrocious tortures, the 49 martyrs of Abitene were killed.

Nine years after the martyrdom of the Abitenes, Constantine freed Christianity.

The year 313 was a turning point for Christianity. After several centuries of persecution by the mighty Roman Empire, the hostilities suddenly ended. The new emperor, Constantine, convinced that his military success was due to the God of the Christians, granted complete freedom of religion to the Christians. He even ordered that the properties stolen from Christians be returned to them.

Further, he spent huge sums of money to build numerous large churches (basilicas) for the use of Christians. The modest house churches—and the occasional simple buildings used for worship during times of peaceful treatment—gradually ceased to exist. Christians were more inclined to choose the basilica model than that of synagogue or temple. While they inherited and reshaped the synagogue liturgy of the word, they now needed a building that would contain a sanctuary and an altar. The temple model did not attract them because the worship took place outside the building and the setting for community inside a building where they could experience themselves more as church was more to their liking.

Interior view of the Aula Palatina, built in the fourth century AD, an early basilica.

The architecture of the basilica is based on ancient Roman law courts. They were rectangular edifices with a rounded space at the far end (called an "apse"), and well suited to the developing concept of public worship. The apse was the perfect place for the chair of the bishop, the altar and the creation of a sacred space for the celebration of Eucharist. Benches were provided for the presbyters. It was customary for the bishop to sit when he preached. Traditionally, recognized wise men sat when they delivered their sage advice, remaining seated due to their great age. This custom was adopted by the bishops who preached the wisdom of Christ. The greatest preachers of the age, Augustine and Chrysostom, sat when they delivered their powerful homilies—and the listeners stood.

A surge of converts from the pagan population brought some details of worship ceremonial from their temples as well as from the rituals of the emperor's court or those of lesser officials. Customs such as kissing

Developing Approved Texts

It is decided that prayers, orations, Masses, prefaces, commendations and imposition of hands that were examined in council may be celebrated by all. No others whatsoever may be used in church—neither those strongly against the faith, nor thought composed by the ignorant, nor those written by the less zealous. Exceptions to this rule are employed by the more skilled or those sanctioned in synod.

—Council of Carthage, AD 407

holy objects as a sign of reverence, genuflecting and the use of incense found their way into liturgy. Signs of honor—bows and incensing—given to the emperor were adapted to gestures that revered the world's true ruler, the Lord God.

ADAPTATIONS

In the imperial cities, Rome, Milan, Ravenna, Alexandria, Antioch, Ephesus and Jerusalem, these new churches appeared. Constantine was even building a new city, Constantinople, with its palaces and Christian basilica. The earliest one, Holy Peace, also called St. Irene's, still exists. The transition to these new centers of worship required careful adaptation. Fortunately, the basic structure of the Mass was in place. For more than two centuries the liturgy of the Word and the importance of the homily had been well developed.

The Eucharistic Prayer, such as the example chronicled by Hippolytus (see pages 35–36), had reached a mature form though celebrants exercised the freedom to insert spontaneous additions. In this new setting bishops decided to standardize the Eucharistic Prayers, now being called a canon.

In the first years the portable wooden table used at home liturgies was used in the basilicas. After a time, these tables were made of stone and marble. The domestic table became the church altar. The stone altar visibly shifted the vision of Eucharist from being a sacred banquet to being a sacred sacrifice. Theologically, the Eucharist was always both, but artistically this change introduced a different emphasis.

Initially, the vast open space of a basilica probably bewildered the bishops and their flocks. The simplicity of the small space of a house is not the same as the grandeur of a building nearly a city block long. It was inevitable that a sense of drama was felt and sought. There should be a proper entrance. Even today it is said, "Everyone loves a parade."

MUSIC

Christians satisfied the need for a suitable entrance with a procession accompanied by music. The simplest way to do that would be the singing of a litany, such as the Song of Daniel (2:20–23). The cantor sang an invocation, "Angels of the Lord," and the people responded with, "Bless the Lord." As litanies multiplied, one of the popular responses was, "Lord, have mercy," (in Greek, "Kyrie eleison"). They also used psalms sung by a cantor or choir, with antiphons used by the assembly.

As the crowds at Mass grew, many of the people were a long distance from the sanctuary. To compensate for this sense of separation, Saint Ambrose of Milan created hymns that all could sing to give the people a sense of solidarity with the priest. Ambrose's hymns were simple, set in stanzas with measured meter. The content was drawn from Scripture and adapted

A manuscript leaf showing the chants to be sung by the choir during Mass.

to the liturgy of the day. His structured hymnody was so successful that it influenced hymn writing for centuries. Some have guessed that in the beginning Ambrose adapted secular songs, perhaps even tavern tunes, for his hymns. Whether this is true or not, what he started is still treasured today as one can observe from the variety of hymns available for Mass.

People regularly sang the Gloria, the Sanctus (Holy, Holy, Holy) and eventually the Agnus Dei (Lamb of God) introduced by Pope Sergius (d. 701). Gradually, professional singers and choirs assumed roles for the chant. The music of this early period has come to be known as Gregorian chant. Scholars argue about whether this is an accurate title, but do agree that music styles such as Old Roman and Old Greek were influential, and to our ears probably sound like what we identify as chant.

VESTMENTS

At house liturgies the bishop or presbyter did not wear vestments. They wore the regular clothing of the day, a little nicer than usual, what we would call their "Sunday best." When the basilicas opened, the celebrants wore the formal clothing of the day. This included an *alb* or floor-length tunic. Over this they wore a *chasuble*—the word means "little house"—which was a conical cloak with a hole in the middle to make way for the head. The front was open at the chest area to give freedom to the hands. Around the neck, they wore a *stole*, a narrow piece of cloth that served as a napkin to clean away dust and sweat from the face and moisture from the hands. No adornments for the head such as mitres for bishops or birettas for priests were used in those days. While the fashions changed, these "lay clothes" were used permanently through the centuries and became sacralized as clerical vestments.

Vestments began as the ordinary clothing of ordinary folk. As secular styles changed, the clergy resisted worldly influences, and eventually these older styles were retained only by the church, which determined uses and wearers. At first vestments were utilitarian, completely lacking in symbolism. The clothing and vessels of the first-century church were the everyday wares of domestic life. The ordinary drinking cup and plate served as chalice and paten, and the longer common tunic served as a sign of civility, because the barbarians wore short garments.[10]

LITURGICAL BOOKS

Once the New Testament was written, Christians could have a whole Bible available for their house liturgies. The Bible was their liturgical book, which they guarded with their lives, both because of the expense of having such a book as well as the threat in times of persecution when police could raid and their treasured Bible taken and burned. After the freedom given by Constantine, the Christians sought to standardize the liturgical prayers. New liturgical books were created and valued, such as the book of Gospels, a lectionary with the annual readings and a sacramentary with the Eucharistic Prayers. Artists decorated the covers with jewels and precious cloths and the pages with miniature paintings, usually of biblical scenes.

One of the advantages of liturgical books was the support liturgical prayers could give to the content of faith when disputes had arisen about the divinity of Christ, the divinity of the Holy Spirit, the truth that Mary was the Mother of God and the truth about the Holy Trinity. The great councils of the church of this period were shaping the correct understanding of the mysteries of faith. It was important that public prayer should echo these teachings and reinforce

The cover of the Samuhel Gospels (circa 1230) is of gilt silver, inlaid with gems, glass and coral.

their acceptance at worship. This led to the axiom, "*Lex orandi est lex credendi*" ("The law of praying is the law of believing").

> Various local synods attempted to regulate the content of liturgical prayers and the books that contained them. A synod in Hippo, attended by Saint Augustine, required that prayers at the altar should be directed to the Father and that prayers borrowed from other places could not be used until they had been examined.[11]

The vessels for holding the bread and wine were originally those made for household use as people brought gifts of bread and wine for Eucharist. One might see a wicker basket for the bread and a wooden or ceramic cup for the wine. In time, this custom was abandoned in favor of gold and silver chalices for the wine and larger gold and silver containers, called *ciboriums,* for the bread.

From the earliest years of the church, it was customary to bring Communion to the sick and the dying using hosts consecrated for that purpose. Eventually a small round gold receptacle called a *pyx* to hold the host was created. In this new era of the church, provisions were made to house leftover hosts in the sacristy. The first record of this custom is found in the fourth-century document, *Apostolic Constitutions.* Saint Basil (d. 379) refers to a vessel that looked like a dove that was used to reserve the Eucharist. We will return to the development of the tabernacle in the Middle Ages and beyond.

THE ROLE OF THE HOMILY

The house liturgies were settings where the scriptural readings for the Liturgy of the Word matured. It became clear that explanations of Scripture were needed and pastoral applications of the Word of God were paramount. The celebration of the Eucharist was the first and foremost place in which this occurred. The early Christians venerated the table of the Word as well as the table of the Eucharist. They hungered for the inspiration of Scripture and the Body and Blood of Christ to which the Bible and the homily pointed. Brilliant saints and holy pastors arose whose prayerful studies and pastoral experience illuminated the Scriptures first at home liturgies and then at the new basilicas

We have come to know them as the Fathers of the church whose eloquence and sanctity flowed from the celebration of the Eucharist. Their voices were heard in apostolic times and throughout the centuries of persecution and in the Constantinian era and for many years after the fall of Rome in 476. Occasionally they taught at learning centers such as the one in Rome where Justin Martyr (c. 100–c. 165) defended the faith at his school for philosophers and the one at Alexandria where Origen (185–254), the church's phenomenal Scripture scholar, expounded the meanings of Scripture.

THE BODY OF CHRIST MAKES THE BODY OF CHRIST

While the Fathers are best known for defending the faith and courageously shaping the correct understanding of the fundamental doctrines of Christianity in the face of powerful assaults from the Gnostics, Donatists and the Arians, their arduous writings and homilies were tied to the dominant theme that held everything together: The Body of Christ in the Eucharist makes the Body of Christ which is the church. Their writing desks were never far from the altar. Their private rooms for thinking were

On Reverence in Receiving Communion

[M]ake your left hand a throne for the right, as for that which is to receive a king. And having hollowed your palm, receive the Body of Christ, saying over it, "Amen." Then, after having carefully blessed your eyes by the touch of the holy Body, consume it—carefully lest you lose any portion. For whatever you lose is evidently a loss to you as it were from one of your own limbs. Tell me, if anyone gave you grains of gold, would not you hold them with all care, on your guard against losing any. Will you not keep watch more carefully, then, that not a crumb fall from you of what is more precious than gold and precious stones?

—Saint Cyril of Jerusalem (315–386)

never distant from the immense challenge of maintaining the unity of the church, which is drawn from the unifying power of the Eucharist.

For nearly three hundred years, between the Last Supper and Constantine, the Christians were welded into a community by their intimate contact with the celebration of the Eucharist. The one sure fountain that bound them together year after year was the refreshment they obtained by proximity to the Bread of Life and the Wine of Salvation in Christian homes.

Their experience of the church was exactly the answer to Saint Paul's forthright challenge to the Corinthians, "Because there is one bread, we who are many are one body, for we all partake of the one bread" (1 Corinthians 10:17). They had little doubt that they were the one loaf, a united body of Christ. On each Lord's Day that unifying force was available to them and building them up into a strong and unified church.

One of the first descriptions of Christians at worship lifts up their hearts to the dream of unity caused by the Eucharist:

> Just as the broken bread was first scattered on the hills, gathered and became one, so let your Church be gathered from the ends of the earth into your kingdom, for yours is the glory and power through all ages.[12]

When the liberated Christians left their house churches for the grand basilicas, they brought with them their solidified faith in the connection between the church and the Eucharist. To think otherwise would be alien to their centuries-old experience of the Body of Christ. The church Fathers needed to make sure that this truth never would be forgotten. The massive authority of Augustine who, more than any other church Father, taught the church as the Body of Christ, was quick to bind that reality to the Eucharist.

> If you wish to understand the body of Christ, listen to the Apostle as he says to the faithful, "You are the body of Christ and His members"

(1 Co 12:27). If therefore, you are the body of Christ and His members, your mystery has been placed upon the Lord's table, you receive your mystery. You reply "Amen" to that which you are, and by replying, you consent.... Be a member of the body of Christ, so that your "Amen" may be true.[13]

Augustine also taught that unity is the special characteristic of the Eucharist. The church tries to be what it receives in communion. Further, the unity of Jesus with his members is symbolized by the mingling of water with the wine in the chalice. The Augustine scholar Peter Brown uses a eucharistic image to characterize the way that Augustine prepared his homilies. This is an excellent example of a homilist at Eucharist whose method links the table of word and sacrament.

Augustine was certain of his basic role. It was not to stir up emotion: it was to distribute food. The Scriptural idea of "breaking bread", of "feeding the multitude", by expounding the Bible, an idea already rich with complex associations, is central to Augustine's view of himself as a preacher.

Fifteenth-century portrait of Saint Augustine by Piero della Francesca.

The little boy who had once supplied his "gang" with stolen tit-bits, would find himself, as a bishop, still constantly giving: "I go to feed so that I can give you to eat. I am the servant, the bringer of food, not the master of the house. I lay out before you that from which I also draw my life." As he told Jerome, he could never be a "disinterested" Biblical scholar: "If I do gain any stock of knowledge (in the Scriptures), I pay it out immediately to the people of God."[14]

The rapid expansion of the church in the new era demanded a pastoral strategy that maintained the sense of unity that had prevailed so well in the age of persecution and minority status. Happily, God provided a remarkable number of extraordinary pastors who filled eucharistic celebrations with a flood of homilies that have never been surpassed in vitality and faith and which are read and studied to this day. These writers understood that the people needed constant encouragement to strive for community and that they would be motivated by their life-long contact with the celebration of the Eucharist.

We need to remember that theology was not an academic discipline separated from the Mass. Most of the church's greatest theological minds were pastors: John Chrysostom, Gregory of Nyssa, Athanasius, Basil the Great, Cyril of Alexandria, Leo the Great, Gregory the Great, Augustine, to name a few. In that golden age, theology and Eucharist were joyously bound together. Emperors and peasants, senators and the working class, aristocrats and the poor flocked together to basilicas in Hippo, Constantinople and Alexandria to hear some of the greatest homilies ever delivered.

This took place at liturgies where a seamless garment of word and sacrament fostered the essential unity that should be the fundamental hallmark of the church. In the Eastern church Saint John Chrysostom, faced with a number of divisive issues, was as eager as all the other faithful pastors to strengthen the unity of the church around the table of the Lord.

> For what is bread? It is the body of Christ. And what do those who receive it become? The Body of Christ—not many bodies but one body. For as bread is completely one, though made up of many grains of wheat, and these, albeit unseen, remain nonetheless present, in such a way that their difference is not apparent since they have been made a perfect whole, so too are we mutually joined to one another and together united with Christ.[15]

The Liturgy of the Word, enshrined and explained by the homily, became an occasion for adult spiritual enrichment in the age of the Fathers. Having become an essential part of the Mass, this reverence for God's word, illumined by faith-filled homilies, fed God's people for centuries and prepared them for Eucharist and lifted their hearts to become the witnessing Body of Christ in their time.

We have considered the two principal parts of the Mass, the Liturgy of the Word and the Eucharistic Prayer. Other elements were gradually added to the Mass. In this chapter it seems suitable to consider two well-known sections, the Gloria and the Creed.

THE GLORIA

When did the Gloria become part of the Mass? The first reference to its use is from a decision of Pope Telesphoros (d. 136) that the Christmas liturgy should begin with the song of the angels. The Gloria starts with the words, "Glory to God in the highest and peace to his people on earth." Luke's Gospel (2:14) uses virtually the same words to report the angels' song just after they had announced Christ's birth to the shepherds. The style of the Gloria is like the hymns of the Bible. It is not meas-

Seventeenth-century portrait of Saint John Chrysostom giving alms, by Mattia Preti.

ured like the psalms but suitable for congregational singing as are many of the scriptural canticles. From the beginning, the Gloria has been a congregational hymn. The people were expected to sing it and, in the early church, that was the practice both at house liturgies and later at the basilicas.

As we will see, when the people were gradually separated from active participation in the Mass, the Gloria became the province of choirs. Just after the Renaissance, composers such as Vivaldi created stirring concertlike renditions of the Gloria. But these theatrical appropriations removed the faithful from their own heritage in singing their prayer of praise.

The Gloria praises each member of the Trinity in turn. The Father is worshiped, thanked and praised with titles of Lord, almighty God and King. Then the Lord Jesus is acknowledged as only Son of the Father and Lamb of God and seated at the right hand of the Father. We are guided to ask for mercy and to have our prayer received. The hymn next acclaims Jesus as alone the Holy One, Lord and Most High. Finally, there is a proclamation of the Holy Spirit linked to Jesus and in the glory of the Father.

The repetition of the title *Lord* is significant in this ancient hymn as an echo of the name for God (Yahweh) throughout the Scriptures. How often we will read that "only the LORD is our God"—and each of the letters in LORD are regularly capitalized. The hymn has more to say about Jesus than either the Father or the Holy Spirit. That is due to its origin as an early version of a Christmas carol. The slim reference to the Holy Spirit will be compensated for in the Creed, to which we now turn our attention.

THE NICENE CREED

There are two creeds in use in the church, the Apostles' Creed that was part of a baptismal service in the church at Rome and the Nicene Creed dating from church councils in the fourth and fifth centuries. These creeds were originally meant to be used at baptisms, not the Mass. They were personal professions of faith, stressing "I believe," not the "We believe," of the community at Mass. The Nicene Creed made its way into the Mass in the sixth century.

The Nicene Creed owes its origin to the Council of Nicea in 325 when the council fathers reaffirmed the divinity of Jesus Christ against its denial by the Arians:

> We believe in one Lord, Jesus Christ,
> the only Son of God,
> eternally begotten of the Father,
> God from God, Light from Light,
> true God from true God.

At the same time, the creed reaffirmed the church's faith in the humanity of Jesus: "[B]y the power of the Holy Spirit, he was born of the Virgin Mary and became man." As time passed, it became clear that the divinity of the Holy Spirit was being questioned. At the Council of Constantinople in 381, this was corrected and the creed was given more forceful words about the Holy Spirit as God.

> We believe in the Holy Spirit, the Lord the giver of life,
> who proceeds from the Father and the Son.
> With the Father and the Son he is worshiped and glorified.
> He has spoken through the Prophets.

The words that follow our profession of faith in the Holy Spirit connect the third person of the trinity with our belief in the church with its four marks of identification: one, holy, catholic and apostolic. The creeds are small masterpieces of the expression of our faith. In their simplicity, they are the outcome of long struggles in the early church with people who wanted to change our faith and undermine what we received from God's revelation. Their enormous value for us each week in Sunday Mass is their putting on our lips and in our minds and hearts the principal doctrines of faith that hold us all together. By reciting the creed after the Liturgy of the Word, we say "Amen" to the revelation of God and utter our thanks for the homily that is a servant of the word.

GNOSTICS

A heresy already present in New Testament times, Gnosticism taught that the spirit is superior to the body and that the flesh should be devalued. Because of this view, the Gnostics denied the Incarnation of the Son of God in the womb of Mary. From their standpoint, it was unthinkable that God would take on a human body, something that was totally unworthy of a divine being. The name of this heresy is based on the belief of the adherents that they have received special private knowledge (*gnosis*) and enlightenment from on high.

ARIANISM

In a sense, fourth-century Arianism (founded by a priest named Arius in Alexandria) is a heresy that is the exact opposite of Gnosticism. If the Gnostics taught that Jesus could never be really human, the Arians believed that Jesus could never be God. A man could never be worthy of being united to the divine nature, they reasoned, because that would denigrate the dignity of God. The Arians taught that God created a superior creature called the "logos" who was united to Jesus and made him the greatest of humans.

DONATISTS

The fourth-century Donatists believed that the Christians who caved into the Roman persecutors and denied Christ by worshiping the emperor could not be welcomed back to the Christian church until they were rebaptized. Augustine fought this heresy, arguing that the sacrament of baptism could not be repeated, but that repentance, confession and absolution were sufficient for accepting lapsed Christians back into the church.

THE LITURGICAL CYCLE

Little by little, the early church developed what we know as the liturgical year. It began with the Feast of the Resurrection, which was linked with the establishing of Sunday as the Christian Sabbath and the day on which Christ's rising from the dead would always be recalled. The Sunday would also recall God's creation of the world and of man and woman as well as the day the Holy Spirit came with his gifts of living flame. Central to this theme is the paschal mystery, the salvation of the world through the death and resurrection of Christ.

The actual feast of Easter was set as the first Sunday after the fourteenth of Nisan, the date of the Jewish Passover. Not all agreed, so the Council of Nicea fixed the date for Easter as the Sunday following the first full moon after the spring equinox. There remain differences due to those who follow the Gregorian (Western) and Julian (Russian Orthodox) calendars.

From the beginning, it was thought that some spiritual preparation such as fasting was needed to prepare for Easter. This eventually became a forty-day period that we know as Lent, first noted by a canon of the Council of Nicea. A Triduum (three days) was formed by adding Holy Thursday and Good Friday to the Easter Vigil.

Another cycle developed that focused on the feasts of Christmas and Epiphany. From the middle of the fourth century, there is evidence of Advent, a four-week preparation for these feasts. The Epiphany was first celebrated on January 6 in the Eastern church in the third century. It recalled Christ's manifestation to the world through the Magi, and the manifestation of divinity at his Baptism and at the sign-miracle of the wine at Cana. Christmas was universally celebrated on December 25 by the sixth century.

Besides these, there arose feasts of the martyrs and virgins of the church in the age of persecution. These were expanded through the centuries as new saints were canonized. A number of feasts honoring Mary grew especially after the Council of Ephesus that defended her title as Mother of God. In our current cycle of saints, the apostles' feasts are distributed throughout the twelve months of the year.

THE PRIESTHOOD

Jesus imparted the priesthood to the apostles on Holy Thursday at the Last Supper. After his Ascension and the descent of the Holy Spirit at Pentecost, the apostles led the new Christian communities in the Breaking of the Bread. As time passed, the apostles ordained bishops as their successors who both oversaw the needs of the church and ordained presbyters (priests) to celebrate Eucharist when the communities grew too large for one bishop to reach, or in outlying districts.

The bishops also ordained deacons to assist at Eucharists. Already in
the New Testament we have a record of this development of bishop,
priest and deacon. The role of bishop and priest was well established
by the end of the first century as seen in the writings of Saint Ignatius
of Antioch.

Ignatius was born about AD 35 and is thought to have been a disciple of Saints Peter and Paul or of Saint John. He became the third
bishop of Antioch probably around the year 70 and was martyred in
Rome in 107. As an experienced bishop ruling Antioch even before
the Gospels were published, his letters to prominent churches provide
us with the wisdom of apostolic times and an extrabiblical confirma-
tion of the development of the priesthood. His letter to the Ephesians,
written when he was on his way to martyrdom in Rome, gives us a
vivid account of what he expected to be the ideal relationship of
bishop, priest and people:

> It is fitting, therefore, that you [Ephesians] should be in agreement
> with the mind of the bishop as in fact you are. Your excellent pres-
> byters [priests], who are a credit to God, as suited to the bishop as
> strings to a harp. So in your harmony of mind and heart the song you
> sing is Jesus Christ.[16]

As the church after Constantine expanded from the cities to the towns
and villages, the bishop customarily broke the consecrated hosts and
sent a part to each of the outlying parishes to signify the unity of the
church with the bishop and each other. In our current Mass, the priest
still breaks the host just after we pray the Lamb of God. The act has
lost its symbolism of unity with other parishes or the bishop, but it
remains a sign that imitates what Jesus did at the Last Supper when
he took bread and broke it. The bishops and priests exercised their
ministry of celebrating Eucharist with a strong emphasis on the unity
and community of the whole people of God. In our next chapter we
will see the gradual change in this ideal in the ensuing centuries as

the people's participation in the Mass was separated from bishops, priests and monks.

Profile

A WOMAN OF MYSTERY: EGERIA'S STORY

Sometime around the year 385, a woman named Egeria (also spelled Aegeria) arrived in Constantinople. She was headed for a three-year journey to the lands of the Bible. Traveling at the rate of twenty-one miles a day, the pilgrimage of over twelve hundred miles to Jerusalem would take her eight weeks. Most authors believe she came from Spain. Many think she was a nun, but others believe she was a woman of independent means, sufficiently wealthy to travel great distances and not be caught short of funds.

Egeria is famous for the diary of her experiences in and around Jerusalem in which she wrote detailed descriptions of the rite of initiation of converts into the church as well as the liturgical practices in Jerusalem during Holy Week—or "Great Week" as she called it. We have lost the manuscripts that contain the beginning of her journey, but what we do have starts with her travels in the Holy Land. She addresses the diary to her "sisters." Whether these are nuns or a social group or actually her family we do not know. She seems unique for her times as a woman traveling without a partner, though accompanied by a tour group for safety's sake.

Her experiences of worship practices in Jerusalem are of interest to us. She saw six churches in the holy city, all associated with events in the life of Christ. She followed their custom of reliving the final events of Christ's passion, death and resurrection by visiting the various churches that were associated with these experiences. At each place she heard Scripture readings, hymns and antiphons related to what happened to Jesus there. Virtually all these sites were in walking distance from each other.

In your imagination you can follow Egeria and the whole Jerusalem community walking to Bethany to relive the resurrection of Lazarus, then strolling to the Mount of Olives to cut down palm branches and proceed with hymns into Jerusalem in the footsteps of Jesus on Palm Sunday.

With her, visit Jerusalem's most prominent church, built next to Calvary and the empty tomb. The Eastern church named it the Anastasis (the Resurrection) while the Western church preferred to call it the Martyrium (the Holy Sepulcher). She describes a Mass for Holy Thursday as follows:

> XXV 2. Then, after the dismissal at the martyrium, they arrive behind the Cross, where only one hymn is said and prayer is made, and the bishop offers the oblation (the Mass) there, and all communicate. Nor is the oblation ever offered behind the Cross on any day throughout the year, except on this one day. And after the dismissal there they go to the Anastasis, where prayer is made, the catechumens and the faithful are blessed according to custom, and the dismissal is made.[17]

On Holy Thursday night, follow Egeria and the Jerusalem community to Gethsemane to spend an hour in prayer, remembering Christ's agony. On Good Friday morning, venerate the relics of the true cross, then gather around the hill of Calvary, still open to the skies in those days but surrounded by a wall of stone columns. Think of gazing at Calvary with Egeria and her fellow pilgrims while the Passion of Christ is being read.

On Holy Saturday night, join the exultant Christian community rejoicing over the newly baptized converts and the reception of Holy Communion. On Easter afternoon complete this pilgrimage with a visit to the Church of Sion on the site of the Upper Room where Jesus instituted the Eucharist and appeared to the apostles on Easter night. Like the best of travel writers, Egeria pictures it all for us, not just as a curiosity, but as a living contact with the mysteries of Jesus Christ.

Her diary alerted the whole church to the Jerusalem innovation of uniting history, geography and liturgy, a practice that has nourished Catholic devotion to this day. Her vivid descriptions charmed the imaginations of countless Christians and prompted them to make a similar pilgrimage, or at least to duplicate features of it in their local churches. Seldom has a devotional travel book been more influential than Egeria's.

PRAYER

Loving God, we praise you for the faith of our fathers and mothers from all the ages of Christian history. We thank you for the gift of Egeria's diary that gives us such a faith-filled insight into the worship life of the Jerusalem church of the fourth century. May we renew our faith in the power of the liturgy to form our Christian lives in the name of Jesus Christ our Lord. Amen.

FOR DISCUSSION

1. When Christianity moved from house liturgies to the basilicas, what was lost and what was gained?

2. In the new basilicas, the table from the house liturgy was brought in. In time, this was replaced by a permanent stone or marble altar. How did this affect worshipers' understanding of Eucharist?

3. Saint Ambrose is credited with introducing hymns into the liturgy. Why was that valuable? What is the advantage of hymn singing today?

4. Eventually, choirs were instituted to help with the more complex chants. What impact did this have on participation in the liturgy by the assembly? What is the influence of cantors and choirs on the assembly today?

5. The "vestments" of the bishop and priests and deacons were the ordinary lay clothing of the day. How did they become "vestments"?

6. With the development of liturgical books other than the Bible, the texts of the Mass became standardized. Why was that valuable? In a time of doctrinal controversy, how did this practice support the faith of God's people?

7. The vessels for Mass were originally the ones in the home where liturgy was celebrated. In the basilica they evolved into chalices and patens. What do you learn from this evolution?

8. The homily assumed a greater importance due to the extraordinary pastoral bishops who emerged in the age of the Fathers. Their theology developed in the context of the Eucharist and a pastoral setting such as a cathedral or parish. Why was this such a gift to the church?

9. The greatest theme of the Fathers' homilies was the essential link between Eucharist and church. Their theme was, "The Body of Christ in the Eucharist makes the Body of Christ the church." Why was that such a powerful grace for the church of the first six centuries? Why do we need it today?

10. Why is the weekly confession of faith in the words of the Nicene Creed so valuable for the assembly?

11. Discuss the essential connection between the priesthood and Eucharist.

12. Discuss your impressions of Egeria's diary of the practices of the Jerusalem church, especially the link between history and Eucharist.

chapter four

· · · · · · · · · · · ·

THE
EUCHARIST
IN THE
MIDDLE
AGES

Some disciples: "This saying is
hard; who can accept it?"
Jesus: "Does this shock you?"
—SEE JOHN 6:60–61

Flannery O'Connor, in one of her letters, recalls a visit she
made to another well-known author and former
Catholic. This letter said:

> [W]hen she was a child and received the Host, she
> thought of it as the Holy Ghost, he being the "most
> portable" Person of the Trinity; now she thought of it as
> a symbol and implied that it was a pretty good one. I
> then said, in a very shaky voice, "Well if it's a symbol, the
> hell with it." That was all the defense I was capable of,
> but I realize now that this is all I will ever be able to say
> about it, outside of a story, except that it is the center of
> existence for me; all the rest of life is expendable.[18]

The shape of the Mass in the Western church gradually evolved along
with the rise of a new political power north of the Alps in the Frankish
kingdoms. With the conversion of Clovis (d. 511) to Christianity, we
have the beginning of a Christian kingdom. A series of internal struggles threatened its existence when the rise of Charlemagne (d. 814)

brought about the Carolingian empire and the needed stability for both church and state.

The liturgy in the north contained the basic structure we have already noted in the previous chapter, but added features that arose in the local culture. There had been some influence from the Eastern church since the time of Saint Irenaeus of Lyons (d. 200) who migrated as a missionary from Asia Minor to Gaul.

Celtic missionaries from Ireland introduced the penitential rite at the beginning of Mass. Benedictine monk-missionaries brought the Roman liturgy with them. The nomadic tribes that arrived at regular intervals contributed their reverence for the bones of ancestral heroes, which they carried with them in decorated caskets, a custom transposed by the church into honored relics of Christian saints.

A number of innovations in the liturgy led to the separation of the assembly from the main altar and the emergence of individual piety rather than communal participation in the Mass. Liturgical texts began using "I" instead of "We." The once public recitation of the Eucharistic Prayer (the Canon) became silent. The Host was no longer given in the hand, just on the tongue. Communion was received kneeling rather than standing. The penitential spirit pervaded the Mass and spread to the members of the assembly, making them feel unworthy to receive Communion. Eventually, the decline of the practice of receiving the Eucharist became so severe that the Fourth Lateran Council of 1215 decreed that all Catholics should receive Communion at least once a year during the time from Easter to Trinity Sunday.

The removal of the assembly from participating in the Eucharist was dramatized by the rise of monastic and clerical Masses. This can be seen still in the architecture of medieval monasteries and cathedrals, both Romanesque and Gothic. The altar is separated from the nave, where the congregation assembled, by the choir stalls for the monks or cathedral canons (diocesan priests). Barriers of stone or wood hid the choir and the altar from public view. Communities of monks or canons conducted their own corporate liturgies away from the assembly.

Naturally, the people demanded that their Mass should be more accessible to them. Thus, the side altars were created to satisfy their needs. This development was magnified by the creation of shrine altars to saints whose relics had been obtained by guilds, wealthy families or other groups. These side chapels lined the walls of churches where the sponsors could gather for Masses for their intentions.

One of the results of separating the assembly from the principal celebration of the Eucharist was the loss of a sense of emotion belonging to the Mass. The language of the liturgy caused another problem for the assembly. In Northern Europe the knowledge of Latin either was never acquired by the local inhabitants or it was devolving into a vernacular form. While the educated classes retained training in Latin, most of the rest did not.

People's faith in the importance of the Mass remained, but their emotional connection was severed and depleted by loss of contact with the celebration. Instead of singing the traditional music of the Kyrie, Gloria, Creed, Sanctus and Agnus Dei, the people created devotional hymns to satisfy their desire to identify with the Mass.

Imaginative writers created dramatic interpretations of the parts of the Mass and

Loss of Active Participation in the Mass

Forgotten is the relationship between the sacramental Body...and the Body of Christ which is the church.... [T]he conscious participation of the community in the oblation [sacrifice] of Christ is lost sight of, and with it that approach of the community towards God to which the Sacrament in its fullness is a summons or invitation. Instead the Mass becomes all the more the mystery of God's coming to man, a mystery one must adoringly wonder at and contemplate from afar.

—Joseph A. Jungmann

The Iconostasis in St. Mark's Cathedral in Venice, showing the separation of the congregation from the altar.

the gestures of the priest. Each aspect of the Mass was linked with a scene from the Passion of Christ, something like imposing the Stations of the Cross on the movements of the celebrant, such as comparing his genuflections with the falls of Christ on his way to Calvary. These interpretations had little to do with the actual meaning of the parts of the Mass or the ritual movements of the priest, but they satisfied a longing of the worshipers to feel connected to the Eucharist.

As members of the assembly felt alienated from the celebrant and the community, a sense of privacy arose. A need developed to find personal satisfaction in a religious experience apart from the Mass appeared. Worshipers became preoccupied with relics, processions, pilgrimages, attachments to favorite saints, acts in which they could invest themselves and find some intimacy with God.

These extraliturgical involvements originally were meant to be faith builders in the central treasure of the church, the eucharistic celebration, from which the people would be able to receive the richest graces of God. Sadly, these practices became substitutes for the Mass—not that they stopped people from attending Eucharist but they diverted people's spiritual energies from the Eucharist itself.

Even when the assembly retrieved its Mass from the enclosures in monastic and cathedral choirs, it did not recover its ability to participate actively in the celebration. The concept of the "private Mass" had arrived, meaning that individuals could request that a Mass be offered for a special intention, usually for the salvation of a departed relative or friend. This was also the beginning of offering the priest a stipend for the Mass. Now though this Mass was actually celebrated for whoever was present, it acquired a style of privacy and silence that effectively shut out the participation of the people.

[T]he extreme quietness of the celebration was the most striking thing about the new form of the Mass, and the latter was therefore justifiably described as the "silent" or "read" Mass. The priest read his part in a low voice; the people stood in silence near the altar, separated from it only by the "Communion rail".... Communication between the quietly praying priest and the silent bystanders had been broken; "active participation" had become an illusion. The faithful might pray privately "during Mass," but they did not share vitally in the celebration....[19]

A Poet's Thought

This Food which no hunger can expel,

This Bread which the Spirit has baked in a holy fire.

This liquid which no thirst can destroy,

This is the Wine which the grape of a virgin's womb has brought forth.

—Matthew of Riveaulx

THE REMARKABLE WORLD OF THE VILLAGE CHURCH

Though all of the above is true, there is a factor that needs remembering, namely that 90 percent of all people lived on farms and in tiny villages and seldom traveled more than five miles from where they were
born. The majority of Christians lived in these rural settings "far from
the madding crowd," stubbornly clinging to the ancient faith even in
a context of the changing shape of the Mass.

Their parish churches were generally small and could house about
two hundred people. The pulpits were often ornamented with symbols
of the seven sacraments, sculptures of the four evangelists and images
of the seven capital sins. Near the ceiling by the altar, worshipers would
most likely see the crucifix with John and Mary at its foot.

The front of the altar often contained a sculpture of the Last Supper
and on the back wall as congregants left the church they would see a
fresco of the Last Judgment. The windows contained stained-glass pictures of apostles, saints, prophets and scenes from the Gospels.
Prominent on a wall would be a depiction of Moses carrying the Ten
Commandments. Statues of angels graced the altar rail.

The intimacy of the village church reflected the close-knit faith community that lived in communion with nature and nature's God. This
was a world comfortable with mystery—and sometimes even with the
mystical. Art underpinned the tradition of the faith, and the parish
priest both knew everybody by name and was known by all. If he lived
to a great age, he would have baptized at least three generations of one
family. The catechesis was simple and memorized easily in that oral
culture.

Even as the Mass was privatized, the environment was one of local
communion where all the people lived, laughed, suffered and died
within the awareness and care of all. The bells signaled times of prayer
throughout the day. The liturgy provided the seasons of salvation from
Advent to Trinity Sunday, and the people devised festivals and processions to mark the mysteries of Christ's life, death and resurrection. The

social life of the people centered on the parish church where civic and religious events were welcomed and sponsored.

Wars and plagues occasionally interrupted this tradition-soaked world, but like the crops that reasserted themselves so also did the people of faith rise again. Even the monasteries that dotted the countryside were often small communities of monks and nuns, usually averaging about twenty-five members. Life spans were short, about forty years.

The Mass may have been in Latin and the people may have participated with age-old hymns that satisfied their need to feel God's presence, and maybe the priest had privatized the Mass like those who ministered in the great cathedrals and monastery churches of famous cities, yet there was an intuitive sense of closeness and communal bonding in these rural churches that transcended the evolving liturgical styles.

The people hungered for the Eucharist and drew strength even from just attending Mass during that strange period when going to Communion had declined. The tens of thousands of rural village churches carried the Mass forward through thick and thin. The heart of the Eucharist flourished in that vast world that nurtured faith and was at ease with the mysteries of God.

The New Custom of Focusing on the Host

Only monks, nuns, and priests received communion frequently. The main object of the layman in coming to Mass was to see the consecrated wafer, and for many the climax came when the priest elevated it after the Consecration. A warning bell was rung beforehand to alert the faithful, many of whom would wander around town going from church to church just to be present at the elevation.... This attitude gave rise to various devotions that focused on the host. The entire town would come out on such feasts as Corpus Christi in June, when the priest would carry the host through the town encased in a glittering gold monstrance.

—Thomas Bokenkotter

Finally, though our study is focused on the Eucharist, we should not forget the prominence of the other sacraments in the life of the community. Large farm families were regularly bringing babies to be baptized and children to be confirmed. Young brides and grooms appeared yearly for the sacrament of matrimony. Confessions were heard often and, in a world of early mortality, the sacrament of anointing was a constant. Celebrations of entrances into the religious life were steady, and periodic ordinations to the priesthood were occasions of great joy for the families.

ADORATION OF THE BLESSED SACRAMENT

At Mass it was customary for the priest to genuflect in adoration of the Body and Blood of Christ after the words of consecration. When the celebration of the Eucharist was moved from homes to the great churches, the priest would face the people for the Liturgy of the Word. However, for the Eucharistic Prayer he would face east, the direction of the sunrise, which symbolized the resurrection of Christ and the presence of God. Since prayer and sacrifice were offered to God, it was concluded that the priest should join the people in this attitude. Hence he faced east with his back to the people. He was not being impolite to the congregation; rather he was gathering them with himself into the Eucharistic Prayer and facing toward God to do this. Churches were built so that they were oriented toward the east.

Since the people could not see the consecrated host and cup, they asked him to raise it so they could join him in adoration of the Body and Blood of Christ. As their involvement in the Mass and their taking Communion radically declined, they sought other ways to fulfill their desire to be connected to the liturgy.

The desire to look upon the Lord's body led to a theory of "communion through the eyes," that is, a saving contact with Christ that consisted simply in gazing on him. The priest was asked to keep the host elevated as long as possible; people willingly gave him a larger

Eighteenth-century monstrance, for displaying the consecrated host. Eucharistic adoration is a devotional expression of faith in the real presence.

stipend to do so, or supplied him with assistants who would hold up his arms if he grew weary.[20]

In time, the idea emerged of showing the Blessed Sacrament outside of Mass. In the thirteenth century artists created a "monstrance" (from the Latin *monstrare*, "to show"). This vessel had a circular glass case into which the host would be put for viewing and adoration. The glass casing rested on a stand and was often surrounded with a metal sunburst effect. Devout people were already accustomed to venerating relics of saints, which were exhibited in glass containers mounted in elaborate boxes of precious woods and trimmed with gold and silver and gems. They found these images of faith to be a support for their spiritual lives and prayed to the saints to intercede on their behalf.

How much more important became the showing of the very Body of Christ! This custom drew people to renew their faith in the real presence of Jesus Christ in the host in the aftermath of the heresy of

Nineteenth-century Corpus Christi procession in Russia.

Berengar of Tours (999–1088) who taught that Christ's presence was symbolic rather than real. At the same time, there was a concern that this approach to the Eucharist would separate people even more from the Mass. There was a need to show that adoration of the Eucharist was an extension of the adoration given at Mass and a way of continuing to experience the blessings of the Mass.

VISIONS OF JULIANA OF LIÈGE

When she was sixteen, Juliana (1193–1258) had visions of a bright moon with a dark band running across it. At first she feared this was a diabolical illusion. Then our Lord appeared to her in a vision or a dream and explained the symbol. He said the moon represented the cycle of feasts in the church calendar. The dark band meant that there was still one important feast missing from the annual calendar: one in honor of the Blessed Sacrament.

Juliana eventually became a nun of Mont-Cornillon. For some time she was in no position to do anything about the institution of a eucharistic feast. However, when elected prioress in 1225, she began

Peter Paul Rubens and Studio, Flemish, 1577-1640, *The Defenders of the Eucharist*, circa 1625. Oil on canvas, 171 x 175 inches, SN214. Bequest of John Ringling, Collection of The John and Mable Ringling Museum of Art, the State Art Museum of Florida.

Defenders of the Eucharist, *by Peter Paul Rubens. Saints Augustine and Gregory lead the procession, but turn back toward the monstrance held by Saint Clare. As a representative of the Franciscan order, she walks beside Saint Thomas Aquinas, the author of the liturgy of Corpus Christi. At the rear is Saint Norbert looking heavenward and Saint Jerome dressed as a cardinal and engrossed in reading the Bible.*

to undertake the project. Through her influence, Bishop Robert de Thorate established the Feast of Corpus Christi for the Liège diocese. In 1264 Pope Urban IV, who had been archdeacon of Liège, ordered the feast to be observed throughout the church. This liturgical feast provided the doctrinal foundation for worship of the Blessed Sacrament outside of Mass as well as the essential link between the Mass and this devotion.

> The Catholic Church has always offered and still offers to the sacrament of the Eucharist the cult of adoration, not only during Mass, but also outside of it, reserving the consecrated hosts with the utmost care, exposing them to the solemn veneration of the faithful, and carrying them in procession [Paul VI, MF 56]. (CCC, 1378)

Corpus Christi processions brought the Eucharist out of the church into the city, town and field of the countryside. These were joyful religious festivals in which the Eucharist shown in the monstrance was carried by the priest wearing Mass vestments and proceeding under a festive canopy. Servers and singers bearing lighted candles led the entire community in the procession. Often little girls carrying baskets of rose petals strewed them in the path of the Eucharist. In some areas carpets made of fresh flowers lined the way. Sometimes the members of the procession walked on the flower carpets; other times they walked alongside them. These customs have remained in old Catholic communities, such as in parts of Germany that named Corpus Christi as "sparkling day" (prantag).

After Vatican II these processions and other devotions to the Blessed Sacrament, such as holy hours in which people adored the Eucharist with hymns and prayers and silent devotion, were largely abandoned due to opinions that "popular piety" was unsuited to modernity. While there was a legitimate unease with excesses in some aspects of devotion, it was a mistake to give them up altogether. Fortunately, there is a vigorous return to eucharistic adoration and Corpus Christi processions.

A DUEL OVER THE REAL PRESENCE

It was probably inevitable that a heresy about the Eucharist would occur in the situation where the congregation became spectators at Mass and where the adoration of the Eucharist often took place outside the Mass. Divorced from the life-giving participation in the celebration—and even the reception—of the Eucharist, some people began to wonder about the real presence of Christ in the sacrament. Left to encounter the Eucharist in popular piety apart from the Mass, it is not surprising that eventually misunderstandings about the Eucharist would occur. This in fact happened in the eleventh century.

The debate was framed by two men, Berengar (also spelled Berengarius) of Tours and Lanfranc, the abbot of Bec, a monastery in Normandy.

Berengar and Lanfranc were both born in 1010, and their careers spanned the eleventh century. Berengar died at seventy-eight; Lanfranc died at seventy-nine. Berengar came from a rich family in Tours, was ordained a deacon and was known for his lifelong generosity to the poor. He could count on the protection of his bishop and Geoffrey Martel, the Count of Anjou, when he faced church opposition to his views on the Eucharist. He taught that the Eucharist was only a symbol that pointed to Christ's real presence.

Lanfranc was born in Pavia, became the abbot of Bec and eventually archbishop of Canterbury. He was a lifelong theological adversary of Berengar. He taught that the bread and wine really did become the Body and Blood of Christ. What both men lacked at first were intellectual tools that would clarify the true faith of the church in the real presence. In the first thousand years of

Lateran IV on Transubstantiation

The Fourth Lateran Council in 1215, presided over by Pope Innocent III, introduced the term transubstantiation into official church teaching. "In the Sacrament of the Altar, under the species of bread and wine, his Body and Blood are truly contained, the bread having been transubstantiated into his Body and the wine into his Blood by the divine power." The substances of bread and wine are changed into the substance of Christ's body and blood, while the appearances of bread and wine remain.

Saint Clare's Devotion to the Eucharist

Due to a type of iconography which has been very popular since the 17th century, Clare is often depicted holding a monstrance. This gesture recalls, although in a more solemn posture, the humble reality of this woman who, although she was very sick, prostrated herself with the help of two sisters before the silver ciborium containing the Eucharist (cf. LegCl 21), which she had

*placed in front of the refectory
door that the Emperor's troops
were about to storm. Clare lived
on that pure Bread which,
according to the custom of the
time, she could receive only seven
times a year. On her sickbed she
embroidered corporals and sent
them to the poor churches in the
Spoleto valley. In reality Clare's
whole life was a* eucharist *because,
like Francis, from her cloister she
raised up a continual
"thanksgiving" to God in her
prayer, praise, supplication,
intercession, weeping, offering and
sacrifice. She accepted everything
and offered it to the Father in
union with the infinite "thanks" of
the only-begotten Son, the Child,
the Crucified, the risen One, who
lives at the right hand of the
Father.*

—*Pope John Paul II*

Christian history, there was no formal eucharistic heresy. In New Testament times the Gnostics denied the humanity of Christ and thus implicitly would have denied the bodily presence of Christ in the sacrament, but that issue did not arise.

Berengar initiated the discussion. Though he was ultimately to lose the battle, he did render a service by challenging his opponents to clarify their language about the Eucharist. It took seven synods from 1050 to 1079 to bring Berengar to agree with the church's position and promise to stop campaigning for his point of view.

What did Berengar teach about the Eucharist?

• The bread and wine remain the same after the consecration.
• The consecration does not change the nature of the bread and wine. It makes them sacraments or signs of the Body and Blood of Christ. (His concept of a sign is something that points to another reality different from itself.)
• Faith associates Christ's presence with the bread and wine, which have undergone no change. He clearly came down on the side of the symbolists.

So serious was Berengar's threat to the church's traditional faith about the Eucharist that three popes in the eleventh century became personally involved in resolving the case. In one of his first encounters with church authorities, Berengar watched his writings on the Eucharist burned in a fire and promised to repent. Back home, he soon resumed his regular teachings. By now, his positions were becoming popular among some clergy and laity alike.

In 1065 Lanfranc wrote a refutation that introduced the concept of transubstantiation for the first time. It was an idea borrowed from the philosophy of Aristotle whose writings had become newly available to medieval thinkers. Ultimately, this idea was the one that would most adequately answer the question, "What kind of change takes place in the bread and wine?" This was his answer:

> The material objects on the Lord's Table which God sanctifies through the priest are—by the agency of God's power—indefinably, wondrously, in a way beyond our understanding, *converted to the body of Christ in their being. Their outward appearances and certain other qualities remain unchanged....*What we receive is the very body born of the Virgin, and yet it is not. It is in respect of its being (essential) and the characteristics and power of its true nature. It is not if you look at the outward appearance (species) of the bread and wine.[21]

At first Berengar disagreed. Then at another Synod of Rome (1079), presided over by Pope Gregory VII, Berengar agreed with this statement that the bread and wine are "substantially converted" into the Body and Blood of Christ. At the age of sixty-nine, he finally submitted, made his profession of faith, promised not to teach his own views any longer and retired to the island of Saint-Cosme. He died on the Feast of the Epiphany in 1088. One year later, Lanfranc died at Canterbury. It took seven synods, three popes and the writings of Lanfranc to bring Berengar to this point. Nevertheless, Berengar's teachings had taken hold, and it would be another hundred years before the church could respond effectively and pastorally to their influence.

Profile

SAINT NORBERT DEFENDS THE EUCHARIST

Norbert was born in Xanten, a cathedral town in Germany near the border of Holland in 1080, exactly one year after Berengar submitted to the church. Ordained a deacon as a young man, he resisted becoming a priest and sought a life of distraction and pleasure. During a life-threatening storm, he underwent a religious conversion. After spending a year of reflection in a Benedictine monastery, he became a priest.

He obtained permission from the pope to be a missionary in France where he traveled from town to town, preaching peace to the warlords, moral reform to the clergy and a revival of faith in the Mass to all the people. In 1121 he founded a new religious order, the Canons Regular of Prémontré. From the Rule of Saint Augustine he emphasized the ideal of community in the spiritual formation of priests. From the traditions of the Benedictines, he formed the prayer life of his future priests around the Mass and the Liturgy of the Hours.

After eight years he was elected archbishop of Magdeburg and started a foundation of Norbertines there, which embarked on active missionary work in the surrounding territories. Saint Norbert died in 1134.

Saint Norbert founded his order in the middle of the "eucharistic centuries" of the church. The eleventh century witnessed the lengthy theological dispute about the Eucharist between Berengar of Tours and Lanfranc of Canterbury. The thirteenth century proclaimed the declaration about transubstantiation at Lateran IV in 1215. Urban IV established the Feast of Corpus Christi in 1264. Thomas Aquinas wrote his classic statement on the Eucharist in the *Summa* in 1272.

What the first four councils of the church did for the illumination of the doctrine of the Trinity, the theological reflections of the eleventh to the thirteenth century accomplished for the doctrine of the Eucharist. Here are seven aspects of Norbert's ministry by which he defended the Eucharist in a pastoral manner.

1. Norbert's missionary apostolate, prior to founding his order, centered on the Mass. When engaged in peace missions, he began with Mass and a sermon, followed this with more preaching, exorcisms and peace discussions, and concluded the day with another celebration of the Eucharist, including a final sermon.

2. The first known mission of the order, just four years after its founding, had a eucharistic purpose. The bishop of Cambrai gave the new community the collegiate church and monastery of Saint Michael's in Antwerp with the purpose of bringing people back to a true faith in the priesthood and the Eucharist.

3. Norbert's central role in the Eucharist is evident in that Peter Paul Rubens created six tapestries celebrating the "Defenders of the Eucharist," one of which shows Saint Thomas Aquinas in the center, flanked by Norbert on one side and Saint Clare carrying the monstrance (shown on page 73).

4. Rubens also did a painting of Norbert carrying the monstrance. Norbertine iconography typically shows Norbert holding the monstrance, even though the monstrance did not come into use until the early 1300s. In the custom of his times, Norbert would actually have carried the Eucharist in a ciborium or pyx, as was the practice for all eucharistic processions, such as those for Palm Sunday and the one to the altar of repose on Holy Thursday. These processions preceded the ensuing Corpus Christi ones, which acquired such prominence.

5. Norbertine iconography emphasizes the order's memory of Norbert's pastoral message and practice, which centered on the celebration of the Eucharist as the foundation of his community. This accords with the incarnational emphasis of the high Middle Ages. While the Cistercians and Franciscans expressed this message primarily through devotion to the humanity of Christ, Norbert's order approached the mystery through the sacrament of the Eucharist. As the hymn "Ave Verum Corpus" states, the Body of Christ at the altar is the same as that born of the Virgin Mary.

6. Saint Norbert was aware of the ferment in eucharistic theology and pastoral practice. He was on speaking terms with popes and bishops whose concern about the Eucharist was essential to their vocation and ministry. His mission tours in France would have exposed him to the varied understandings and practices regarding Eucharist.

7. As founder of abbeys in Antwerp and its environs, Norbert encountered Tanchelm's eucharistic heresy. By sending the first mission team of Norbertines to Antwerp to help the inhabitants recover their faith in the real meaning of Eucharist, he won their enduring respect. The ancient Cathedral of Our Lady in Antwerp displays on its whole west wall stained-glass panels of Norbert carrying the monstrance in a Corpus Christi procession.

Saint Norbert did not provide a theological response to the erroneous teachings of Berengar and Tanchelm, but rather a pastoral one. He was a gifted preacher and a talented pastor. He preached the faith of the church in the Eucharist as it was found in Scripture and the homilies of the church Fathers. As a wise pastor, he drew attention to the centrality of the Mass, reintroducing the custom of a homily at Mass and emphasizing the dignity of the celebration by insisting on cleanliness in the sanctuary and reverence in the ceremonies. He also devised a method of training priests through the liturgical life and communal living. What the theologians clarified in their writings, Saint Norbert translated into pastoral practice.

PRAYER

Like Mary, let us be full of zeal to go in haste to give Jesus to others. She was full of grace when, at the annunciation, she received Jesus. Like her, we too become full of grace every time we receive Holy Communion. It is the same Jesus whom she received and whom we receive at Mass. As soon as we receive Jesus in Holy Communion, let us go in haste to give Him to our sisters, to our poor, to the sick, to the dying, to the lepers, to the unwanted, and the unloved. By this we make Jesus present in the world today.[22]

FOR DISCUSSION

1. As you read the history of the Mass in the Middle Ages what goes through your mind when you discover the gradual process of separating the congregation from active participation in the Mass?

2. In reviewing the various steps that led to the gaps between people and priest at Mass, which ones seem the most serious to you? Why so?

3. While the shift to a focus on the consecrated Host was a result of the "new look" of the Mass, what was the benefit for popular piety as a result?

4. How did the feast of Corpus Christi integrate adoration of the Blessed Sacrament with the liturgical celebration?

5. Why has it been said that imposing scenes from the life of Christ on the gestures of the priest and the movement of the ritual at Mass was not helpful for genuine participation in the Mass?

6. In reading the story of the long-standing debate between Berengar and Lanfranc about the real presence of Christ in the Eucharist, what relevance to our own times have you noticed?

7. How might the practices of popular piety that are related to the Eucharist enhance our appreciation of the Mass?

8. What was the impact of the village church on the faith of rural parishioners?

9. After reflecting on the profile about Saint Norbert, can you identify the essential actions he took to defend the Eucharist? What has surprised you about him?

10. Why is it important to remember that medieval Christians not only had a wealth of popular piety, but also a vivid sacramental life with baptisms, confirmations, weddings, anointings, ordinations and confessions as well as Eucharists?

chapter five

• • • • • • • • • • •

THE MASS IN THE TIME OF THE REFORMATION AND COUNTER-REFORMATION

The Lord Jesus himself declares: *This is my body*. Before the blessing contained in these words a different thing is named; after the consecration a body is indicated. He himself speaks of his blood. Before the consecration something else is spoken of; after the consecration blood is designated. And you say, "Amen," that is: "It is true." What the mouth utters, let the mind within acknowledge; what the word says, let the heart ratify.
—FROM THE TREATISE ON THE MYSTERIES BY SAINT AMBROSE

On October 31, 1517, Martin Luther posted ninety-five theses on the door of the castle church in Wittenberg. He was challenging his academic peers to a debate on the subject of the sale of indulgences. No one showed up for the debate, but copies of his theses circulated throughout Germany and touched off a religious firestorm. Luther had initiated the Protestant Reformation that was to divide church

The Mass as a Sacrifice

The Mass is a sacrifice inasmuch as it makes present in a sacramental and unbloody manner the sacrifice of Jesus Christ at the cross. This is a mystery of faith that reveals to us the generosity of Christ in making available through the Holy Eucharist his ultimate saving act at Calvary at each Mass. Hence the graces of the cross become available to the faithful at every Eucharist.

Through the ministry of the ordained priest, Christ makes it possible for the members of the Christian assembly to offer to the Father a perfect sacrifice that is Christ himself, pleasing in every way and able to bring forth countless blessings.

affiliation in Europe and eventually the rest of the world.

On December 13, 1545, thirty bishops arrived in the Italian city of Trent to open an ecumenical council. The Council of Trent would last eighteen years, though it was in session only about four years. The Council fathers first addressed the doctrinal challenges posed by Luther and then created reforms that affected the pastoral life of the church.

Their first order of business was to dispel confusion about Catholic teachings. On matters of doctrine, the Council of Trent taught that Scripture and Tradition are foundational for the church. It denied that faith alone is sufficient for salvation. Hope and charity are also necessary. In Catholic practice, the virtue of love in cooperation with God's grace should result in good works.

The Council reasserted the ancient faith of the church in the truth of the seven sacraments, the real presence of Christ's Body and Blood in the Eucharist and that the sacrifice of Christ is made present in the Mass. It affirmed the divine institution of the priesthood and retained the concept of transubstantiation as a way of explaining how Jesus is present in the Eucharist. It also upheld the visibility of the church as an institution founded by Christ and built on the rock of Saint Peter, whose successors are the popes, and the apostles, whose successors are the bishops. Related to this issue they recognized the supremacy of the pope.

PASTORAL NEEDS

The Council also issued decrees designed to revitalize the pastoral life of the church. Bishops were ordered to stay in their dioceses and priests in their parishes and shepherd their people. The sale of indulgences and clergy jobs was forbidden. The Council called for the creation of seminaries and outlined principles for the proper education and formation of future priests. It abolished the practice of priests offering a number of private Masses each day just to collect stipends.

Finally, the Council commissioned the completion of a universal catechism that had been started in 1563, and authorized a committee to reform the liturgy of the Mass and the Breviary. In that era when the ties to the church were crumbling, everywhere there was a perceived need to do everything possible to unify the ecclesial community.

For this purpose they elected a pope who was fully equipped to implement these pastoral decisions of the council. That man was Pope Pius V (1566–1572). Made of stern stuff, he was a man for his times. A disciplined ascetic all his adult life, he wore his rough Dominican habit under his papal robes. He imposed strict standards on everyone around him and reduced the size of the papal court. Within his first year as pope, he issued the *Roman Catechism.*

Despite the angry temper of the times, this catechism was not polemical—filled with attacks on Protestants—nor expressly controversial. It aimed to present Catholic truth clearly, attractively and comprehensively rather than refute the errors of the times. It became an enduring sourcebook for teaching religion up to its last edition in 1979.

Soon, short question-and-answer catechisms appeared. They were adaptations of the *Roman Catechism* written by Saint Peter Canisius for German-speaking peoples and by Saint Robert Bellarmine for southern Europeans. They were standard texts for religious education of children and adults up until modern times. (The *Baltimore Catechism* was an heir of these works.) Their importance for liturgy was fulfilled by giving students doctrinal explanations of the Mass, Holy Communion and the other sacraments.

It should also be noted that many dioceses published sermon outlines that covered a three-year cycle. These outlines were drawn from the *Roman Catechism* and followed its sequence of creed, sacraments, morality and prayer. In this way, the priests became familiar with the Catechism and the people were given a doctrinal foundation for their faith life.

Pius V then published the new Roman Missal in 1570. Pius decreed that the Missal would be the standard book for Mass in the Western church, thus restoring the unity and dominance of the Latin Rite. He believed that uniformity of the texts was absolutely necessary, though some exceptions were made for dioceses that had liturgical customs dating back two hundred years. The rubrics (rules for liturgical behavior) were clear and unambiguous. The people were not expected to participate; they were treated as reverent spectators.

Everything pertained to the priest-celebrant and his action at the altar, including the Liturgy of the Word. The participation of the people was devotional rather than liturgical. They sang hymns that usually had little to do with what was happening as Mass. The Scripture was read in Latin and little understood by its listeners. The sermon usually was not about the readings.

Eucharistic adoration normally occurred outside the Mass, but sometimes there was exposition of the Blessed Sacrament during Mass. People seldom went to Communion, which often was not distributed during Mass and sometimes totally apart from Mass, leaving the impression that Communion was not an integral part of the celebration of Eucharist. One reason why this reform of the liturgy was inadequate was a lack of knowledge of the history of the Mass. Other than what was described at the Last Supper, most students did not have available a history of the evolving shape of Eucharist from apostolic times up and through the age of the early Fathers when active participation in the Mass by the people was essential and expected.

Also, the demands of overcoming the chaos left by the Reformation as well as numerous abuses that needed correction left the church leadership with little time and energy to do or sponsor the research. The chaos required crisis management and that was what happened. Still, the Mass of Pius V, also known as the Tridentine Mass, was a sturdy worship event that endured virtually unchanged for four centuries until the revisions of Vatican II. Millions of Catholics around the world found that this Mass provided a source of global identity and a sense of belonging to the universal church.

THE CHURCH AS THRONE ROOM—THE BAROQUE

During the early years of the seventeenth century, the church had recovered its balance and experienced a surge of energy. It found a way to express its vitality in a new architectural image first tried by the Jesuits. The remarkable contributions of the new Jesuit order, known for its centralization, flexible mobility and dynamic presence, built its new mother church in Rome, the Gesu, in what became known as *Baroque* architecture. The name comes from a term that describes a pearl of irregular shape.

The altar in the chapel of the Sagrario illustrates the Baroque notion of the church as throne room.

In this new type of church, the choir stalls are removed and the screens and walls that hid the choir are done away with. The sanctuary is visible once again, and it is shortened so that it is easily seen by the congregation. Side aisles that had been obstructed by a forest of pillars are gone. The altar is against the wall, which is now lavishly decorated—from floor to ceiling—with a sunburst of color manifested in sculptures of Christ, the Father and the Spirit, angels, saints and mythic figures curved and often seemingly poised in flight. The impact is dramatic and emotional.

An imposing tabernacle rests on the altar. Midway up the wall is a spacious niche designed for exposition of the Blessed Sacrament. The side walls continue the theme of vivid colors and sculptures of biblical figures seeming to be in constant movement. Most churches avoided stained-glass windows, preferring clear glass to take advantage of the light needed to accent the demands of Baroque art.

A soaring pulpit was situated near the middle of the church, indicating that preaching was once again a major feature of the liturgy, though the substance of the sermon was seldom the readings of the Mass. Here is a worship space that glows with self-confidence, victory and strength. It suited the mood of the Counter-Reformation church and became its architectural signature. It was a building that reassured the assembled congregation that the church had survived an extraordinary crisis and was forging ahead with missionaries headed for the New World and to Asia.

> Baroque style used exaggerated motion and clear, easily interpreted detail to produce drama, tension, exuberance, and grandeur from sculpture, painting, literature and music....The popularity and success of the "Baroque" was encouraged by the Roman Catholic Church when it decided that the drama of the Baroque artists' style could communicate religious themes in direct and emotional involvement.[23]

Yet, hidden in all this splendor was the altar; unspoken was the fact that the invisible wall separating the people of God from active participation in the Mass was still firmly in place. The Mass remained the province of the priest. Moreover, the Mass was often celebrated during the exposition of the Blessed Sacrament—placed in the large niche halfway up the back wall and amidst the expanse of religious statuary around it. It was a throne. In time, this custom was to be discontinued.

The sanctuary had become a stage and the people, now seated in pews, were the audience. The church had become a throne room for God. To make these comments is in no way meant to withdraw honor and adoration for the Blessed Sacrament nor to deny the value of enthroning the Real Presence. What we have here is a matter of discernment and proportion. The Mass should be central act of the church's worship in which priest and people unite, each according to their role.

At the same time, we should not forget that our forebears of this period kept the faith and passed it on eventually to us. The Holy Spirit was at work in the church, producing many saints and countless numbers of holy witnesses to Christ. They had the seven sacraments and loved and adored the Holy Eucharist. They loved and venerated

The Table of the Word and the Table of the Eucharist

I acknowledge my need of two things—food and light. You have therefore given me in my weakness Your sacred Body to be the refreshment of my soul and body, and have set Your Word as a lamp to my feet. Without these two, I cannot rightly live; for the Word of God is the light of my soul, and Your Sacrament is the bread of my life. One might describe them as two tables, set on either side of the treasury of holy Church. The one is the table of the holy altar, having on it the holy bread, the precious Body of Christ; the other is that of the divine law, that enshrines the holy doctrine, teaches the true faith, and unerringly guides our steps even within the veil that guards the Holy of Holies.

—Thomas à Kempis, The Imitation of Christ

our Blessed Mother and honored the saints. They raised their children in the faith, said their prayers and looked out for the poor.

Further on in this chapter, we will reflect on the great teachers of the spiritual life of this period who trained millions in the art of prayer. Religious orders sired an army of missionaries who accompanied immigrants to the United States and ministered to their sacramental needs. They built cathedrals in the jungles of Latin America and sailed to India, Japan and China. Everywhere they brought the cross and the Eucharist and the charity of Christ.

One of the great treasures the people of this period possessed was a culture permeated with Christian ideals. This was true in Protestant as well as Catholic nations. Historians refer to this notion of the world as a kind of Christian society based on common values as Christendom. They did not experience the challenge we face today, a culture that is progressively secularized, making it difficult to maintain our faith. They had their saints and sinners—just as we do. But their secret weapon was a culture that reminded them of the ages of faith where memories of God were visually present to them and near-universal attitudes that supported their beliefs.

Though we cannot help but view their liturgical life through the lens of our own blessings, we should not anachronistically project the present on the past. The mysterious ways in which God remained present to his people should invite us to take a humbler stance when we attempt to judge other times. We have our own shortcomings and blind spots that will be noted long after we are gone. We would like to think our descendants will be gentle with us.

PREACHING

The prominence of the great pulpits in Baroque churches indicated that preaching had become more important once again. We have already seen that priests were encouraged to preach at Mass and that they were provided with outlines from the *Roman Catechism*. In practice, this meant that one year they would give sermons on what was termed the twelve articles of the creed, following the topics of God the Father and the work of creation, the Fall of man and the promise of redemption. This led to reflections on Jesus Christ as Son of God, born of the Virgin Mary and who saved us by his death and resurrection. Next, the sermon cycle would discuss the work of the Holy Spirit and then the church, with its four marks, followed by preaching on the belief in the resurrection of the dead and the life to come.

In the second year, priests would preach on the seven sacraments, what each one meant, the requirements for reception, the graces conferred and their rela-

The Jesuit Church (Jesuitenkirche) in Vienna boasts a pulpit richly decorated in the Baroque style.

tionship to salvation. They would most likely also spend time on the sacramentals, especially in a time when popular piety flourished.

Finally, in the third year they preached on the Ten Commandments, their origin, what virtues they teach and what sins are forbidden by these commandments. This would be in the context of the great commandments of Jesus to love God above all and one's neighbor as oneself. At some point in the year, the Beatitudes would also be treated.

The priests could supplement these topics with encouragement to practice the spiritual and corporal works of mercy, how to avoid the seven capital sins and how to live the virtues of faith, hope, charity, prudence, justice, temperance and fortitude. The numerous feasts of the Blessed Mother and the saints also provided them with sermon opportunities and exhortations to prayer and acts of piety.

Given the controversial nature of the times, priests taught their people the details of Catholic doctrine, especially on issues where it differed from Protestant beliefs. In German-speaking countries that used the catechism of Saint Peter Canisius—a book that expressly refuted Protestant claims—sermons would assume a similar approach.

This model of preaching was not formally connected to the readings of the day, though examples from the Gospels would naturally be used when they corresponded to the assigned topic. Still, this was not scriptural or liturgical preaching.

In each generation of the four centuries from Trent to Vatican II, gifted preachers arose. Some were founders of religious congregations, such as Saint Alphonsus Liguori, who wrote and preached dynamically on Christian morality, or Saint Francis de Sales, whose sermons were models of restraint and filled with appealing examples and stories that motivated the listeners to prayer and virtue. The Jesuits, who stressed education, were gifted in teaching Catholic doctrine and life through their sermons, and in their missions they excelled at sermons that drew the listeners to conversion to Christ and the church.

Not all preaching occurred at Mass. From the Middle Ages onward, the Franciscans and Dominicans preached in public squares or large cathedrals, both educating people about the faith as well as calling them to moral and spiritual conversion. After the Council of Trent, members of other religious orders and congregations joined in this practice, which developed into what was called "parish missions," for Lenten reflections, novenas or preparation for great public feasts. These were occasions of spiritual renewal, comparable to the religious revivals conducted by Protestants. The preachers addressed the need to confess one's sins, to do penance and to resolve to follow Christ more ardently.

CHURCH MUSIC

Some of the best church music ever written began in a prayer room where a priest called "God's clown" was converting Rome's elite. His name was Saint Philip Neri (1515–1595). He had established a good-sized oratory, or prayer room, for his afternoon seminars and institutes on Scripture, spirituality, church history and the lives of the saints. There would normally be four sessions of speeches and discussions interspersed with prayer and music. He had an instinctive love of quality music and understood the value of singing to promote a sense of community.

Philip attracted some of the best musicians in Rome to his oratory. He encouraged them to compose hymns, songs and madrigals based on dramatic stories from Scripture, such as the dialogue of Jesus with the woman at the well. Philip insisted that many of the lyrics be in Italian so that the people could understand them. He also asked them to write in simple melodic lines to make sure that the words could be heard clearly.

At that time, church music was in just as sorry a state as everything else was. One was liable to hear hymns that were little more than sentimental love songs containing allusively erotic themes with no reference to Christ or divine meaning. At other times, one might hear hymns, whether humanistic or divine, submerged by deafening organ music and drums, so that the texts could not be heard.

Choral Masses

I have found to my astonishment that the Catholics, who have had music in their churches for several centuries, and sing a musical Mass every Sunday…do not to this day possess one which can be considered even tolerably good, or in fact, which is not actually distasteful and operatic…. Were I a Catholic, I would set to work at a Mass this very evening; and whatever it might turn out, it would at all events be the only Mass written with a constant remembrance of its sacred purpose.

—Composer Felix Mendelssohn

*The Cantual of Mainz (1605)
borrowed an idea from Luther and
allowed the substitution of German
hymns for the proper of the Mass.
By the eighteenth century, hymns
were permitted in some places as
substitutes for the ordinary of the
Mass. This Singmesse gave the
people a new sense of
participation.
—Edward Foley*

In Philip's oratory, musical geniuses such as Animuccia and Palestrina began the rejuvenation of church music, creating the "Renaissance polyphony" that became one of the glories of ecclesiastical music. In their vernacular settings of dialogues from Scripture, they created musical plays, an idea that was later adopted by Handel for his *Messiah*, Haydn for his *Creation* and Bach for his *Saint Matthew's Passion*. The oratorios of the great master Protestant musicians all had their origins in the oratory of Philip Neri. It was from his prayer room that the name and style of that musical form originated.

The music of Palestrina, sung without instrumental accompaniment (a cappella), is still a major part of Vatican liturgies, especially those in the Sistine Chapel where no organ is allowed and only a capella singing is permitted. It evokes a transcendent feeling and moves the listener toward God. It was used widely during the early period of the Baroque churches. Newer composers such as Mozart and Haydn also composed music for the ordinary parts of the Mass. In the operalike setting of Baroque churches, these Masses seemed at home. Of course, this somewhat transformed the liturgy into a "concert," further keeping the congregation in a spectator mode.

The Protestants developed a vast number

of hymns, based on Scripture, easy to understand and suited to congregational singing. Luther understood how effective a good hymn
could be in teaching a scriptural lesson. Even Bach's cantatas, a new
one for every Sunday of the year, although requiring a trained choir to
sing, were written in the spirit of the hymns—or chorales, as they were
called. They were deeply scriptural and understandable and took
advantage of music's ability to touch the heart. Catholics also wanted
hymns and, in time, their desire was satisfied.

Toward the end of this period of history, there was a revival of
Gregorian chant. In addition, the Saint Cecelia school of music arose to
replace the operatic and concert-style Masses. The result was a return to
a more sober and restrained type of Solemn (or High) Mass in which
choral music was sung and the celebrant was assisted by priests who
functioned as deacon and subdeacon.

THE IMPORTANCE OF SPIRITUALITY

In conjunction with the Tridentine Reformation, a new type of
Catholic spirituality appeared that was to remain the standard for the
following centuries. The Tridentine decree on justification stressed
the importance of good works—exerting a decisive influence on the
direction taken by this spirituality in the modern era. It meant that
Catholics would conceive a spiritual perfection as involving a high
degree of personal activity—combining an active striving after self-
control, the acquisition of virtue, a zeal for the good works of mercy
and charity.... A science of meditation originated, which became one
of the most important tools used by Church leaders in the reform of
clergy and laity.[24]

Though it has always been true that the graces of God have been
drawn from the celebration of the Eucharist in which the whole treasure of the church exists, nevertheless, the capacity to receive these
graces was related to the ways in which the communicant prepared for
Mass. Just showing up for Mass without any prior prayer life or active
pursuit of virtue or a self-awareness of one's relationship with Christ

normally meant that the person arrived at Eucharist unprepared to receive the blessings offered.

A modern version of this deficiency is the complaint, "I don't get anything out of Mass." To some extent, this is a mechanical view of the role of Eucharist in one's life. Not only is the soul constricted by little exercise of the life of faith, but also it is open to so little at Mass that its subsequent impact is minimal. The response to the complaint is "What do you bring to church? Who is the you that arrives in the pew? What kind of conscious spirituality and prayer go on between attendance at Masses?" Of course, it must also be said that the celebrant and ministers should lead a liturgy that is warm, inviting and inspiring— including the homily.

This issue was brilliantly addressed in the years after the Council of Trent. Giants of spirituality sprang up and flooded the church with schools of meditation, mysticism and programs of spiritual growth. Saint Ignatius led the way with his Spiritual Exercises, whose effectiveness has rarely been surpassed and remains today one of the best practical approaches to spiritual development. Ignatius found a way to surface human energies in the cause of self-discipline and meditation, while ever upholding the primacy of God's graces.

The Carmelite doctors—Teresa of Avila, John of the Cross and Thérèse of Lisieux—wrote books that analyzed mystical states or, as in the case of Thérèse, left a spiritual autobiography that was remarkably accessible to millions. To this day Carmelite cloisters of nuns and monasteries of friars are centers of prayer for the church and the spiritual needs of many.

Saint Francis de Sales excelled in providing a human touch in his spiritual direction of the laity, pointing them toward the love of God and showing them how to live a devout life in everyday circumstances. One of his disciples, Saint Vincent de Paul, brought this message to the numerous parish missions that he and his teams conducted, but above all to the formation of priests in seminaries. For centuries now, seminarians have been trained not only in theology, but also in meditation and the acquisition of virtues. Thousands of bishops and priests were trained to spend time in meditation before Mass to sharpen the capacity of their souls to receive the graces Jesus would give them.

Of course, it was not just the immediate preparation for Eucharist that counted, but also the remote preparation through the exercises of the spiritual life. These efforts at spiritual development were already present in the Benedictine and Cistercian traditions as well as those started by Saint Francis and Saint Dominic.

There is no way here we can cite all the saints and religious communities who were fed with these schools of spirituality and in turn fed others. The vast army of religious sisters and brothers were formed in this period and brought the fruits of that formation to their students in schools and to their patients in hospitals.

A Catholic instinct was at work in all of this: that the purpose of spiritual development was directed at deriving from the Mass the full impact of what Christ wished to impart. It was always the Mass that mattered. It is also interesting to note that confession and Communion became more frequent in this period, though there were setbacks caused by Jansenism, which inculcated an excessive sense of guilt in people (see more on Jansenism on pages 98–100).

It is worth repeating that these schools of spirituality were not just used by priests and religious, but by the laity in huge numbers. Thousands of laypeople found a meditative repose in adoration of the Blessed Sacrament. The increased practice of the Forty Hours devotion and Benediction of the Blessed Sacrament strengthened this link between contemplation and being present before the Sacrament. Gradually, it was widely accepted that a lively spiritual and moral life expanded the capacity of the soul to receive the abundant graces of the Eucharist.

Profile

SAINT MARGARET MARY (1647–1690)

> Christ loved the church and gave himself up for her, in order to make
> her holy by cleansing her with the washing of water by the word, so
> as to present the church to himself in splendor, without a spot or
> wrinkle or anything of the kind. (Ephesians 5:25–27)

Around the time that Margaret Mary Alacoque was born, a dangerous
and false teaching arose in Belgium. It spread through France and
Holland and was to linger in seminary training for many years. It was
proposed by Bishop Cornelius Jansen who wrote a book on what he
believed to be the teachings of Saint Augustine, but what were actually misinterpretations of those teachings. Jansen argued that we do
not have free will and that we are unable to resist temptation, hence
we are unable to keep all the commandments.

He further maintained that Christ did not die to save everyone, and
only the most worthy have the right to receive Communion. He felt
there was too much attention paid to Christ's humanity and that his
followers should practice severe penances. These teachings burdened
many people's consciences and often caused the growth of obsession
about one's moral guilt. The Jesuits fought these ideas, and the movement was condemned by Pope Clement XI (1700–1721).

Born in Burgundy, Saint Margaret Mary would have an important
role to play in repudiating Jansenism. Her father died when she was
eight; she was sent to school at the convent of the Poor Clares. Two
years later, she contracted a rheumatic condition that confined her to
bed until she was fifteen. As she neared the age of twenty, her family
pressured her to get married, but she had long felt a calling to be a
nun. She finally entered the Visitation convent at Paray-le-Monial in
June 1671.

On December 27, 1673, while she was at eucharistic adoration, she received the first of a number of private revelations from Christ. He told her that the love of his Sacred Heart for all people needed to be made known everywhere. She should be the messenger of the boundless love expressed in his heart. Over the next eighteen months, he appeared to her and communicated to her the meaning of what he had revealed.

Jesus taught her that people ought to become aware of his love and be invited to enter into a loving communion with him. He said that the faithful should be encouraged to go to Communion frequently (and especially on the first Friday of each month) and to make an hour's vigil before the Blessed Sacrament in memory of his hour in Gethsemane. Catholics were to make this devotion through a series of nine First Fridays and the Holy Hour. Lastly, Jesus asked her to promote a Feast of the Sacred Heart for the Friday after the octave of Corpus Christi. Today, these feasts are on succeeding Sundays.

As normally happens to those who claim personal visions and messages from a heavenly being, there is a long discernment process to test the authenticity of the revelation. Margaret Mary would face the same demanding process, experiencing the doubts of her superiors and of the theological experts brought in to investigate the matter. Finally, her new Jesuit confessor, Blessed Claude de la Colombière, was convinced of the truth she spoke and he defended her and the call from Jesus Christ to have people believe in the treasures of his love that flowed from his heart. The Jesuit order popularized this devotion within its Apostleship of Prayer.

The content of this private revelation was nothing new, for the love of Christ had been made manifest from the moment of his incarnation. Saint Paul exulted in this truth about Christ:

> But God, who is rich in mercy, out of the great love with which he loved us even when we were dead through our trespasses, made us alive together with Christ—by grace you have been saved—and

raised us up with him and seated us with him in the heavenly places in Christ Jesus, so that in the ages to come he might show the immeasureable riches of his grace in kindness toward us in Christ Jesus. (Ephesians 2:4–7)

This celebration of the love of Christ was the perfect tonic for the pessimistic and soul-destroying doctrine of the Jansenists. The devotion increased Mass attendance and the reception of Communion and re-awakened in Catholic hearts the original teachings of the Gospels, that is, the ultimate reason the Son of God came among us proceeded from a motivation of infinite love that invites our love in return (see John 3:16–17).

PRAYER
Father, we rejoice in the gifts of love we have received from the heart of Jesus your Son. Open our hearts to share his life and continue to bless us with his love.[25]

FOR DISCUSSION
1. When you read about the challenges faced by the church during the Reformation, both from within and without, how might this help you cope with the challenges facing today's church?
2. What do you think of the decision of the fathers of the Council of Trent to commission a universal catechism?
3. The Council of Trent issued a number of doctrinal clarifications about the Mass, both in response to the views of Protestants and to problems with the liturgy of the day. Why was it important to make the doctrine on these issues clear?
4. When you read about the details of Baroque architecture, what went through your mind? If you belong to a church with contemporary architecture, what occurs to you in comparison to the Baroque? If you belong to a church that has more traditional architecture, how does the architecture help or hinder your participation in the Mass?

5. Catholics in the centuries just before modern times lived in a Christian culture. What does that mean? Why was that a strong support for their faith?

6. When you review the section on the method of preaching in seventeenth and eighteenth centuries, with its outlines on the creed, sacraments and morality, what do you think are the positive and negative aspects of such an approach?

7. Baroque churches lent themselves to elaborate choral Masses, some written by great composers such as Mozart. How do you feel about this approach to church music? What do you think of church music today?

8. Review the rise of schools of spirituality in this period. Do you think it fair to say that those trained this way would be more open to the work of the Holy Spirit at Mass?

9. What do you think of the teachings of Jansen? Is the devotion to the Sacred Heart of Christ's love a good response to Jansenism?

10. By now you should have some sense of the many stages in the development of the Mass. How is this helpful to you?

chapter six

· · · · · · · · · · ·

THE
MASS
IN THE
ERA OF
VATICAN II

"[W]e... have come to pay him homage."
—THE MAGI (MATTHEW 2:2)

"Adoration is not a luxury; it is a priority."
—POPE BENEDICT XVI

Vatican II was a dramatic turning point in the history of the Mass.

The actual ceremony of the promulgation [of the Constitution on the Liturgy] began with the solemn chanting of the Creed.... Pope Paul knelt at the faldstool and recited the conciliar prayer.... We are here present, Lord Holy Spirit.... After the Pope had intoned the Veni Creator Spiritus [Come, Holy Spirit], the secretary general began the truncated reading of the text of the Liturgy Constitution and the ballots were collected. Some ten minutes later Archbishop Felici approached the pope with the results and announced an overwhelming majority of 2,147 favorable to 4 opposed. Thereupon the Holy Father rose together with the bishops and pronounced the solemn formula making this an official document of the Church…: "We approve (this Constitution) together with the Fathers."[26]

THE ROOTS OF THE RENEWAL OF THE MASS

At least a hundred years before the event cited above, the stirrings of liturgical change had begun. Dom Prosper Guéranger and the monks of Solesmes Abbey in France initiated the revival of Gregorian chant and historical studies of the development of the liturgy. The members of the abbey were able to recover Gregorian chant melodies and restore their original form and rhythmic structure. They published the results in a chant hymnbook called the *Liber Usualis* that became widely influential.

Guéranger also wrote a series of volumes entitled *The Liturgical Year.* It was an informative and readable catechesis of the texts of the Roman liturgy both for the Advent, Lenten and Easter cycles as well as for Ordinary Time and the feasts of saints and was a popular commentary right up to Vatican II.

In Germany the Benedictine abbeys of Maria-Laach and Beuron pursued similar interests, especially liturgical art in the style of the icons of the Eastern church. Dom Odo Casel of Maria-Laach wrote *The Mystery of Christian Worship*, in which he provided a persuasive argument for involvement in the liturgy, understood from the faith perspective of the celebrations of the Christian mysteries. He did more than simply call for behavioral change at Mass; he opened up the spiritual depths of the saving power of the liturgy. He drew attention to the central and solemn importance of the Easter Vigil and actually died at the vigil while joyfully singing the "Exultet" (the hymn about the Easter candle).

In 1909 an international conference on the liturgy was held at Malines, Belgium. Dom Lambert Bauduin delivered a paper on the importance of active participation of people in the Mass. His speech is traditionally thought to be the official inauguration of the liturgical movement.

The writings of these pioneers influenced the formation of seminarians in religious congregations and dioceses and the training of nuns and a number of the educated laity. They received a boost from the interest of Saint Pius X who wrote about the need to revitalize church music, especially Gregorian chant, as well as to lower the age for reception of First Communion to seven. In encouraging frequent Communion and the singing of chant, the pope fed into the growing pressures to involve congregations in the Mass. Gradually, a number of parishes in Europe, the United States and elsewhere taught their people to sing the tuneful Gregorian *Missa de Angelis* (Mass of the Angels) with relative ease.

Despite two world wars, hyperinflation in Germany and the Great Depression everywhere else, the energy to reshape the liturgy continued enthusiastically. In Austria, Father Pius Parsch of the canons of Klosterneuberg wrote a five-volume series of well-informed meditations on the Mass and the Divine Office. His approach was prayerful and pastoral, appealing not just to priests and religious, but also to the laity. He sowed the attitudes that drew people into an inspiring spirituality that flowed from liturgical life.

At Saint John's Abbey in Collegeville, Minnesota, Dom Virgil Michel became a national leader of the liturgical movement. His challenging editorials in the abbey magazine, *Orate Fratres* (now named *Worship*) nourished his readers with the results of liturgical research in Europe as well as the ways to relate liturgy and life. He showed people how to link liturgy with the call to Christians to apply their faith to the social order of politics, economics and the needs of the poor. His fellow Benedictine Godfrey Dieckmann followed the same trail.

Other writers for *Orate Fratres* included Monsignor Martin Hellriegel of St. Louis and Monsignor Reynold Hillenbrand of Chicago. Hellriegel was born and raised in Germany and experienced some of the fresh winds of liturgical renewal. At age seventeen he entered Kenrick Seminary in St. Louis. As a nun's chaplain and later pastor of Holy Cross parish in St. Louis, he found many ingenious ways of applying the new thinking to the celebration of Mass and the flow of the liturgy. He had a folksy German style and a flair for poetic imagery. He preached the new liturgy at numerous priest retreats and national congresses.

One of his favorite topics was the Roman custom of having a procession to a different ancient church—named a stational church—for Mass for each day of Lent. He showed how the history of a given church, its patron saint and the selected texts formed a unity and a source of growth in faith for the participants.

Monsignor Hillenbrand provided excellent columns on the impact of the doctrine of the Mystical Body for a proper participation in Mass and was also skilled in showing people how social and moral responsibility was the desired outcome of going to Mass. Another regular columnist for *Orate Fratres* was H.A.R. (the *R* stood for "Reinhold") who had the knack of evaluating the state of worship, its understanding and its potential in dioceses and parishes. For many readers his contributions were the highlight of their monthly copy of the magazine.

Certainly a giant of the liturgical movement was the Jesuit Joseph Jungmann whose magisterial *The Mass of the Roman Rite*, probably did more than any other study to foster an educated appreciation of how the Mass fared from the Last Supper up to the days before the Second Vatican Council. In this work, his footnotes are a treasure, filled with countless examples of liturgical practices—the good, the bad and the unhelpful.

Among all these pioneers, Romano Guardini excelled at revealing the inner mystery of the liturgy and the inward spiritual attitudes we need to truly live the call of liturgical celebration. Some people are beguiled by the externals of the liturgy, the music, vestments, precious vessels, architecture, poetry, ceremony and pageantry. Guardini warned that unless we are drawn by this symphony of color, form and enchanting movement into the reality to which they point, we will forever remain at the threshold of the visible and never encounter the invisible majesty of our Lord Jesus Christ waiting there to meet us and sanctify us. Guardini's book *The Spirit of the Liturgy* is his masterpiece and is as relevant now as it was when he wrote it. Following is a sample of his thought concerning the link between liturgy and truth:

> To participate in Holy Mass means to recognize Christ as the Logos, Creator, and Redeemer. "As often as you shall do these things, you should do them in remembrance of me." Remembrance here does not mean only: "Do this to commemorate me." It means in addition: "While doing this, think of me, of my essence, my tidings, my destiny; all these are the Truth." It is not by accident that the essential action of the Mass is preceded by the Epistle and Gospel, for each of the sacred texts is a clue to Christ's identity, is some facet of His personality or truth, some event in His life that comes forward to be understood or accepted. Each is a ray of that Truth which will be present at the Consecration no longer in word but in His real existence.[27]

A powerful support for the liturgical movement came from the encyclical Mediator Dei by Pope Pius XII. His statement that the primary source of the Christian life comes from active participation in the liturgy of

The Truth of the Mass

It is of primary importance that we see Truth's relation to the Mass. Piety is inclined to neglect truth. Not that it shuns it or shies away from it, but it is remarkable how [in] reality piety slides off into fantasy, sentimentality, and exaggeration. Legends and devotional books offer only too frequent and devastating proof of this; unfortunately piety is inclined to lose itself in the subjective, to become musty, turgid, unspiritual. Divine reality is never any of these, never falsely spiritual in the sense of the vaporous, the insubstantial. Divine reality, which is another name for truth, remains as divinely substantial as the living Jesus who walked the earth. But it must be illumined by the spirit, the Holy Spirit.

Truth is essential to the fullness of the Mass. It is not enough to harp on the fact that the Mass is the center and content of the Christian's life. It must also be made clear how that center may be reached and that content shared. This is possible only when truth's vital relation to the Eucharist is recognized and when truth permeates the entire act of the sacred celebration.

—Romano Guardini

the church became a watchword for all people seeking the renewal of the liturgy. The pope provided a useful survey of the development of liturgy from the Council of Trent up to his own time. He emphasized the need for a proper interior spirit at Mass, the centrality of the Holy Eucharist and continued promotion of the doctrine of Christ's real presence in the Eucharist.

RESHAPING THE MASS

After the Second Vatican Council, liturgical change occurred but the substantial structure of the Mass remained unchanged. The first part

still retained an Opening Prayer, readings from Scripture and a Homily. The Gloria and Credo were kept for Sundays and feasts. The Offering of Gifts, the Preface and the Canon of the Mass with its major parts (Invocation of the Spirit, Words of Institution, Remembrances and so on) were also retained. The Our Father, the Communion service, the Closing Prayer and the Blessing were also preserved.

This image of Cardinals Frings, Spellman and Gerlier, taken in 1950, is illustrative of the traditional garb prevalent before the Second Vatican Council.

Gone, however were the opening prayers at the foot of the altar, the silent reading of the Canon, the shifting of the Sacramentary from one side of the altar to the other by a server, the wearing of a biretta by the priest, bowing one's head at the name of

Jesus, the singing of hymns that had no relationship to the liturgy, people praying the rosary silently during Mass, the so-called Last Gospel (John 1:1–14) and the devotional prayer to Saint Michael the Archangel, "low" Masses offered with no solemnity, solemn high Masses with vested deacon and subdeacon (usually priests) and a choir singing the ordinary parts of the Mass.

Gone, too, in many places were the statues of saints, the vigil lights, the sound of the bells during the consecration, realistic representations of the passion in the Stations of the Cross, stained glass windows that had recognizable pictures of biblical scenes or portraits of saints.

However, a number of changes were introduced.

A priest wearing garments representative of post–Vatican II styles.

The priest now faced the people, illustrating the dialogical aspect of the Mass as well as his presiding role. The use of the vernacular instead of Latin was introduced. People now shook hands at the gesture of peace. The congregation was asked to participate actively in the Mass, to sing and pray at various times.

With the departure of Latin, oddly and sadly, Gregorian chant suddenly disappeared, even though many congregations sang in Latin quite well and knew what the words meant. On the positive side, people discovered the wealth of hymns used in the Protestant churches

Christ's Presence in the Eucharist Is Greater Than in the Assembly
Pope John Paul II, in his 2003 encyclical on the Eucharist, said that we should be able "to recognize Christ in His many forms of presence, but above all in the living sacrament of his body and blood." There is a vast difference between Christ's presence in the Eucharist and in the assembly of its members. The worshipers, if they have the proper dispositions, are mystically united to God by grace. The Holy Spirit dwells in them, but they retain their own personal identity. They are not transubstantiated; they do not cease to be themselves and turn into Christ the Lord.
—Cardinal Avery Dulles

and some fine contemporary hymns such as "O God Beyond All Praising," based on a melody from Gustav Holst's *The Planets.* On the negative side, a raft of newly composed sentimental songs were adopted, some of which failed not just to be good music, but also lacked a sound theological basis and were somewhat self-congratulatory instead of being praises of God.

The worshipers were invited to receive Communion either in the hand or on the tongue and to stand during its reception. They were also offered the chalice so they could communicate under both species. To help with Communion, laity and religious could serve as extraordinary ministers of the Eucharist. Married deacons appeared who not only assisted the celebrant at Mass but could preach the homily too. Priests stopped wearing the old "fiddleback" vestments and adopted chasuble styles that traced their lineage back to Roman times. Entrance and offering processions were added.

The Mass readings now included one from the Old Testament, one from the New Testament letters, Acts of the Apostles or the book of Revelation, and a reading from a Gospel. This new system of readings was divided into cycles A, B and C, each one lasting a year, thus assuring that the congregation would hear large portions of

Scripture in a sequential manner. In many cases, whole books are read.

Church architecture in new suburban areas, compared to that of the old city churches, was austere, plain, minimalist in decoration and functional. Altar rails fell away and the congregation was brought close to the altar. Instead of the rectangular, pillared shoebox of times past, now there was half-moon shaped auditorium that had good sightlines to the altar and made people feel close to the ritual.

However, there is a newer trend taking place in which churches reflect traditional styles such as American colonial, Hispanic Southwest adobe and ancient Romanesque (without the pillars). These churches do not slavishly copy old styles, but adapt them to contemporary needs and use the blessings of technology for sound, light, heat and cooling. The Norbertine parish church Holy Rosary in Albuquerque, New Mexico, is an example of this trend in the style of Pueblo Revival. Statues have returned, but attractively in a bevy of midsized niches in the walls surrounding the seating area. The design of the statues adapts the traditional art of New Mexico—colorful and iconic.

The baptismal font, often obscured in older churches, now occupies a prominent place either at the entrance to the building or in the roomy sanctuary. Choir lofts are gone and the choir has been moved to a space near or even in the sanctuary. Organs are supplemented with guitars, pianos, electronic instruments and even small bands or orchestras.

Modern lighting brightens the worship space. A simple lectern replaces the elaborate pulpits of olden days and technology provides sound systems to help the preacher speak in a conversational tone and still be audible. The tabernacle has been removed from the altar and relocated to a separate altar either in the sanctuary or in another chapel. A number of new churches include attractive gathering spaces for visiting before and after Mass, a detail very desirable in cold climates where the weather often makes such "community building" difficult.

The range of change has been a bit breathtaking and many parishes have gone over the top in experimenting. The speed at which this dismantling took place caused what Alvin Toffler called "future shock," except it happened in the here and now. Many people were confused, scandalized and alienated and so walked away. Most people muddled through and stayed with the church though regular weekly Mass attendance declined from 70 percent to 40 percent. It should be added here that liturgical change was not the only cause of the losses of church attendance; other causes included difficulties in catechesis and the rising divorce rate, the breakup of families, materialism and sexual license and what some consider to be the general secularizing of culture.

THE ESSENTIAL ELEMENTS OF THE NEW EUCHARISTIC CELEBRATION

Having reviewed the details of changes in the Mass and the liturgical settings, it is important to note what has finally emerged. Gradually the benefits of the direction given by the council fathers at Vatican II along with a series of liturgical directives from Pope Paul VI, Pope John Paul II and the Congregation for Divine Worship, the dust settled and the clear outline of the shape of the new Mass became clear. We may speak of this revised form in terms of five essential movements:

1. *The Gathering.* The assembly normally gathers at a parish church. Jesus, our high priest, invisibly presides over the celebration. The bishop or priest is the visible presider, acting in the person of Christ, preaching the homily and saying the Eucharistic Prayers. All the worshipers are called to prayer, to actively participate in the liturgy: deacons, readers, servers, those who bring up the offerings, the extraordinary eucharistic ministers—and the whole assembly whose "Amen" signifies their participation. The ritual of gathering includes the Entrance Procession and accompanying music, the greeting of the people, the penance prayer, the Gloria and the Opening Prayer.

2. *Liturgy of the Word.* There are readings from the Old Testament and from the New Testament: the epistles of the Apostles, the Acts, the

book of Revelation and the Gospels. The Homily and the Intercessory Prayers follow the readings. The proclamation and explanation of the Word of God is a call to deeper faith in Jesus Christ and prepares the people for the next part of the Mass. The texts of the Bible—the book of Christ—are not simply literary writings of various prophets and apostles. They are the words of the living Christ spoken to us just as truly as when he walked about Galilee speaking to our ancestors in the faith.

3. *The Presentation of the Offerings.* Normally on Sundays there is a procession in which the bread and wine is borne to the altar. This remembers Christ "taking the bread and wine" and changing it into his Body and Blood. This is also a good time to offer ourselves to God in union with the sacrifice of his Son. From the days of the early church, there were also offerings of food and money for those in need. Hence, the collection for the needs of the parish and other worthy causes happens at this time.

4. *The Eucharistic Prayer.* This section of the Mass has six parts:

Preface. We thank the Father through Christ and in the Spirit for the gifts of creation, salvation and sanctification. This helps us recall that the word *Eucharist* means "giving thanks." Everyone joins the priest in saying or singing the praises of the angels, "Holy, Holy, Holy."

Epiclesis (Invocation). We ask the Father to send the Holy Spirit to change the bread and wine into the Body and Blood of Christ through the ministry of the priest.

Institution Narrative. The acts of the Spirit and Christ give power to the words spoken by the priest to transform the bread and wine into Christ's Body and Blood. Only validly ordained bishops and priests may do this. This part concludes with the celebrant inviting the people to proclaim this mystery of faith with words such as, "When we

The Eucharist Causes the Unity of the Church

The church is not born as a simple federation of communities. Her birth begins with one bread, with the one Lord.... She becomes one not through a centralized government but through a common centre open to all, because it constantly draws its origin from a single Lord, who forms her by means of the one bread into the one body. Because of this, her unity has a greater depth than that which any other human union could ever achieve. Precisely when the Eucharist is understood in the intimacy of each person with the Lord, it becomes also a social sacrament to the highest degree.

—Pope Benedict XVI

eat this bread and drink this cup, we proclaim your death, Lord Jesus, until you come in glory."

The Remembrance. We remember the passion, resurrection and glorious return of Christ. In the context of the Mass, this is more than recalling events that happened centuries ago. The Mass is a memorial that makes present the one sacrifice of Christ and the spiritual benefits of salvation from sin and the graces of divine life achieved for us by Christ.

Intercessions. We are joined by the whole communion of saints in heaven and earth and we ask our heavenly friends to pray for our needs and for those who have died. More things are wrought by prayer than this world dreams of. Our concern for each other begins with prayer and is followed up by action whenever possible. At Mass, we invoke the prayers of the most powerful saints who ever lived, above all the Blessed Virgin Mary. Jesus Christ—the one mediator between God and us—is present on the altar. But he brings his heavenly court with him so that we have the fullness of what we need spiritually.

Communion. After the Lord's Prayer and the breaking of the bread, we receive the Body and Blood of Jesus Christ. The liturgy is the place to meet Jesus. Christianity is not simply an idea. The Mass is more than a holy classroom. The church is more than a system of thought as though it were a book to be mastered. The essence of our religion and Mass is a person—Jesus Christ, Son of God, Son of Mary and Savior of the world. We do not receive pages of a text. We receive a live person, in fact the very source of life itself.

5. *The Commission to Live the Mass.* The Mass closes with the final prayer and the blessing of the assembly and the commission to live this Mass in our daily lives: "The Mass is ended. Let us go in peace to love and serve the Lord and one another." We have heard Jesus speaking to us personally. We have met him in Communion where he changes us into his likeness, to think and love as he did and to let him be vitally present to the world through our lives. Our faith in his real presence in the Eucharist has been strengthened. He is truly real. He wants us to be truly real also, and his transforming grace makes this possible. When our presence is real, we say what we mean and we mean what we say. The union in us of what is seen and unseen is truly real when the two sides are the same.

The Mass Is Our Life and Work

But there is also the attempt made by some young priests to reach the young, to make the Mass meaningful to the young (the bourgeois, educated, middle-class young), where novelty is supposed to attract the attention but which, as far as I can see, has led to drawing these same young ones completely away from the "people of God," "the masses" and worship in the parish church. There is the suggestion of contempt here for the people and for the faith of the inarticulate ones of the earth.... I do love the guitar Masses, and the Masses where the recorder and flute are played, and sometimes the glorious and triumphant trumpet. But I do not want them every day, any more than we wanted the Gregorian Requiem Masses every day. They are for the occasion. They are joyful and happy Masses indeed and supposed to attract the young. But the beginning of faith is something different. "The fear of the Lord is the beginning of wisdom. Fear in the sense of awe."

—Dorothy Day

Profile

MARY, "WOMAN OF THE EUCHARIST"

The following words are from Pope John Paul II's *Ecclesia de Eucharistia:*

> If we wish to rediscover in all its richness the profound relationship between the church and the Eucharist, we cannot neglect Mary, Mother and model of the church. In my Apostolic Letter *Rosarium Virginis Mariae*, I pointed to the Blessed Virgin Mary as our teacher in contemplating Christ's face, and among the mysteries of light I included the *institution of the Eucharist*. Mary can guide us towards this most holy sacrament, because she herself has a profound relationship with it.
>
> At first glance, the Gospel is silent on this subject. The account of the institution of the Eucharist on the night of Holy Thursday makes no mention of Mary. Yet we know that she was present among the apostles who prayed "with one accord" (cf. Acts 1:14) *in the first community which gathered after the Ascension in expectation of Pentecost.* Certainly Mary must have been present at the Eucharistic celebrations of the first generation of Christians, who were devoted to "the breaking of bread" (Acts 2:42).
>
> But in addition to her sharing in the Eucharistic banquet, an indirect picture of Mary's relationship with the Eucharist can be had, beginning with her interior disposition. *Mary is a "woman of the Eucharist" in her whole life.* The Church, which looks to Mary as a model, is also called to imitate her in her relationship with this most holy mystery....
>
> What must Mary have felt as she heard from the mouth of Peter, John, James and the other apostles the words spoken at the Last Supper: "This is my body which is given for you" (Lk 22:19)? The body given up for us and made present under sacramental signs was the same body which she had conceived in her womb! For Mary,

receiving the Eucharist must have somehow meant welcoming once more into her womb that heart which had beat in unison with hers and reliving what she had experienced at the foot of the Cross.

"Do this in remembrance of me" (Lk 22:19). In the "memorial" of Calvary all that Christ accomplished by his passion and his death is present. Consequently *all that Christ did with regard to his Mother* for our sake is also present. To her he gave the beloved disciple and, in him, each of us: "Behold, your Son!". To each of us he also says: "Behold your mother!" (cf. John 19:26–27).

Experiencing the memorial of Christ's death in the Eucharist also means continually receiving this gift. It means accepting—like John—the one who is given to us anew as our Mother. It also means taking on a commitment to be conformed to Christ, putting ourselves at the school of his Mother and allowing her to accompany us. Mary is present, with the Church and as the Mother of the Church, at each of our celebrations of the Eucharist. If the Church and the Eucharist are inseparably united, the same ought to be said of Mary and the Eucharist. This is one reason why, since ancient times, the commemoration of Mary has always been part of the Eucharistic celebrations of the churches of East and West.

In the Eucharist the Church is completely united to Christ and his sacrifice, and makes her own the spirit of Mary. This truth can be understood more deeply by *re-reading the Magnificat* in a Eucharistic key. The Eucharist, like the Canticle of Mary, is first and foremost praise and thanksgiving. When Mary exclaims: "My soul magnifies the Lord and my spirit rejoices in God my Saviour", she already bears Jesus in her womb. She praises God "through" Jesus, but she also praises him "in" Jesus and "with" Jesus. This is itself the true "Eucharistic attitude."[28]

PRAYER

Had I but Mary's sinless heart,
To love Thee with, my dearest King.

O! with what bursts of fervent praise
Thy goodness, Jesus, would I sing!
Sweet sacrament, we thee adore!
O make us love thee more and more!

FOR DISCUSSION

1. For those of you who remember the Mass before Vatican II, how did you react to the changes? What are your thoughts about the Mass today?

2. For those of you who never experienced the Mass before Vatican II, what are your thoughts about the Mass you do experience?

3. Now that you have read about the history of the Mass and its many developments, what struck you most? Why is it valuable to know the ways in which the Mass was celebrated in different periods of history?

4. How are you motivated now to participate in the celebration of the Eucharist with a living, conscious and active faith?

5. If asked, what would you suggest concerning the music at Mass, that is, the use of the organ or other instruments, the choice of hymns, the role of the cantor, the participation by the people?

6. As you listen to homilies at the liturgy of the Word, what would you like to suggest to the homilist regarding the length of the presentation, its relevance to daily life, its use of pertinent examples, the interpretation of Scripture, doctrinal content, the quality of preparation, the degree of inspiration?

7. What else would you like to know about the Holy Eucharist?

8. How do you see the Eucharist affecting your daily life and your Christian commitment to love, mercy, justice and peace?

9. If you have spent time in adoration of the Blessed Sacrament what would you say to encourage others to do this?

10. When you reflected on Pope John Paul's invitation to "go to the school of Mary" for deeper appreciation of the Eucharist, what helped you most?

conclusion

· · · · · · · · · · ·

One conclusion we can reach from this short history of the Mass is that changes in the liturgy, whether large or small, have been occurring regularly. The basics have never changed, but the details, decisions by church authority, and the attitudes of the participants have undergone modifications and development. In this sense, the celebration of the Eucharist is a dynamic and living reality. While a constant diet of experimentation is not healthy or desirable, a loving attention to the quality of the divine celebration is a necessity. We need to avoid both frivolity and stagnation. In recent times there has appeared a hunger for ways to express reverence at liturgy, a wholesome refining of the attitudes of the assembly at Mass. New needs will arise in the years ahead. Yet the noble core of the Eucharist from the Upper Room to an urban cathedral or a village church has withstood the tumults of history—and always will.

notes

· · · · · · · · · ·

1. John Paul II, *Ecclesia de Eucharistia*, 2.

2. Roman the Cantor, *Glimpses of the Church Fathers: Selections from the writings of the Fathers of the Church*, Claire Russell, ed. (London: Scepter, 1994), p. 476.

3. "O Jesus, Joy of Loving Hearts," text attributed to Bernard of Clairvaux, para. by Ray Palmer, tune WAREHAM, LM; William Knapp. (Chicago: GIA, 1986), number 605.

4. John Paul II, Holy Thursday Letter to Priests, 1985, 1.

5. Saint Augustine, Sermon 34, 1–3, 5–6. Quoted in Office of Readings for the third week of Easter.

6. John Paul II, Apostolic Letter *Mane Nobiscum Domine*, 3, 11, 19.

7. Joseph A. Jungmann, s.j., *The Mass of the Roman Rite: Its Origins and Development* (New York: Benzinger Brothers, 1950), p. 18.

8. *Didache*, 9, quoted in Johannes H. Emminghaus, *The Eucharist: Essence, Form, Celebration*, Matthew J. O'Connell, trans. (Collegeville, Minn.: Liturgical, 1978), p. 26.

9. Justin Martyr, *First Apology*, 67, quoted in Emminghaus, p. 36.

10. Barbara Dee Baumgartner, *Vestments for All Seasons* (Harrisburg, Penn.: Morehouse, 2002), p. 4.

11. Edward Foley, *From Age to Age*, Robin Faulkner, illus. (Chicago: Liturgical Training Publications, 1991), p. 57.

12. *Didache*, 9, quoted in Emminghaus, p. 26.

13. Augustine, Sermon 272, available at http://www.webcam.creighton. edu/fileadmin/user/ministry/StJohns/docs/Girm/j-GIRM_03-The_Body_of_Christ.pdf.

14. Peter Brown, *Augustine of Hippo* (Berkeley, Calif.: University of California Press, 1967), p. 252.

15. Saint John Chrysostom, Homily on First Corinthians, 24, 2. Available at http://www.zenit.org/english/viualizza.phtml?sid=34382.

16. Letter to the Ephesians by Saint Ignatius of Antioch, quoted in Liturgy of the Hours, volume III, p. 80.

17. From Louis Duchesne, *Christian Worship: Its Origin and Evolution* (New York: E. and J.B. Young, 1903).

18. Flannery O' Connor, *The Habit of Being,* p. 125. Quoted in James T. O'Connor, *The Hidden Manna: A Theology of the Eucharist* (San Francisco: Ignatius Press, 2005), p. 95.

19. Emminghaus, p. 76.

20. Emminghaus, p. 81.

21. Lanfranc, "Body and Blood of the Lord," pp. 18-19, quoted in Roman R. Vanasse, ed., *Reclaiming Our Norbertine Heritage* (DePaul, Wis.: St. Norbert Abbey, 1995), p. 79.

22. Blessed Mother Teresa of Calcutta. Available at http://www.thereal presence.org/eucharst/tes/quotes9.html.

23. http://en.wikipedia.org/wiki/Baroque, p. 1.

24. Thomas Bokenkotter, *A Concise History of the Catholic Church* (New York: Image, 2005), p. 230.

25. From the liturgy of the Feast of the Sacred Heart.

26. Xavier Rynne, *Vatican Council II* (Maryknoll, N.Y.: Orbis, 2002), p. 262.

27. Romano Guardini, *The Spirit of the Liturgy* (New York: Herder and Herder, 1998).

28 . Pope John Paul II, *Ecclesia de Eucharistia.*

index

• • • • • • • • • • •

illustration credits

• • • • • • • • • • •

Page 4, Duccio (di Buioninsegna) (c. 1260-1319). The Last Supper. Panel from the back of the Maesta altarpiece. Location: Museo dell'Opera Metropolitan, Siena, Italy. Photo credit: Scala / Art Resource, NY.

Page 12, The Tassilo Chalice, a gift from Duke Tassilo II of Bavaria and his wife Liutpirc to the Abbey. Gilded copper with niello Carolingian, c. 770 CE. Location: Abbey, Kremsmuenster, Austria. Photo credit: Erich Lessing / Art Resource, NY.

Page 28, Entrance of the Synagogue of Capernaum, Israel. (Late 2nd or early 3rd CE). Location: Synagogue, Capernaum, Israel. Photo credit: Erich Lessing/ Art Resource, NY.

Page 32, Caravaggio, Michelangelo Merisi da (1573-1610) The Supper at Emmaus. Location: National Gallery, London, Great Britain. Photo credit Nimatallah/Art Resource

Page 34, Burial niches with fresco of Christ Pantocrator. Location: Catacomb of S. Callisto, Rome, Italy. Photo Credit: Erich Lessing / Art Resource, NY.

Page 43, Interior view of the Aula Palatina. Roman, 4th CE. Location: Palastaula, Trier, Germany. Photo credit: Vanni / Art Resource, NY.

Page 45, Antiphonary in note 7 (H), a book which contains the chants to be sung by the choir during Mass. Initial "D" of Dulce; Heraclius returns the cross to Jerusalem. Latin Manuscript, Gothic writing, second half 14th. Parchment, 56 x 38 cm. Galbandian. Location: Studium Biblicum Franciscanum, Jerusalem, Israel. Photo credit: Erich Lessing / Art Resource, NY.

Page 47, cover of the Samuhel Gospels. Quedlinburg, Germany. 1225-1230. gilt silver, precious stones, glass, pearls, corals, eye-of-pearl. Photo: Ann Muenchow. Location: Treasury, collegiate Church St. Servatius, Quedlinburg, Germany. Photo credit: Bildarchiv Preussischer Kulturbesitz / Art Resource, NY.

Page 51, Piero della Francesca (c. 1420-1492). Saint Augustine. Location: Museu Nacional de Arte Antia, Lisbon, Portugal. Photo credit: Scala / Art Resource, NY.

Page 53, Preti, Mattia (1613-1699). St. John Chrysostom giving alms. Location: National Museum of Archaeology, La Valletta, Malta. Photo credit: Scala / Art Resource, NY.

Page 66, Masegne, Jacobello dalle (fl. 1383-1409). The Iconostasis, 1394. Location: S. Marco, Venice, Italy. Photo credit: Erich Lessing / Art Resource, NY.

Page 71, Monstrance, 18th CE. Location: Dioezesanmuseum, Bamberg, Germany. Photo credit: Scala / Art Resource, NY.

Page 72, Prianishnikov, Ilarion (1840-1894). Corpus Christi Procession in the Kurski District. 1893. Oil on canvas, 101.5 x 165 cm. Photo: Roman Beniaminson. Photo credit: Bildarchiv Preussischer Kulturbesitz / Art Resource, NY.

Page 73, Peter Paul Rubens and Studio, Defenders of the Eucharist, bequest of John Ringling, Collection of The John and Mable Ringling Museum of Art, the State Art Museum of Florida.

Page 87, Altar in the Chapel of the Sagrario. Location: Cathedral, Segovia, Spain. Photo credit: Erich Lessing / Art Resource, NY.

Page, 91, Jesuitenkirche (Jesuit Church) in Vienna. 1627. Altered by Andrea Pozzo in 1703-05. Interior with pulpit. Location: Jesuitenkirche (Jesuit Church), Vienna, Austria. Photo credit: Vanni / Art Resource, NY.

Page 108, © Getty Images, Photo by Fox Photos / Stringer.

Page 109, © The Crosiers / Gene Plaisted, O.S.C.